Experts Praise *Girl to Girl*

"*Girl to Girl* is an engaging resource for girls going through puberty. Sarah O'Leary Burningham addresses the wide range of emotional and physical changes that girls experience in a way that is comprehensive, fun, and caring."

—Mark A. Schuster, MD, PhD, William Berenberg Professor of Pediatrics at Harvard Medical School, Chief of General Pediatrics at Boston Children's Hospital, and co-author of *Everything You Never Wanted Your Kids to Know About Sex (But Were Afraid They'd Ask)*

"Ever wish you had a smart, savvy, cool big sister to give you the inside scoop on your changing body and emotions? Sarah O'Leary Burningham delivers! Practical and confidence-building, she covers everything from taking care of your changing hair and face, to a great how-to for learning to shave your legs. Going through puberty leaves some feeling alone and confused. *Girl to Girl* leaves girls feeling understood and self-assured."

—Alan Greene, MD, Pediatrician, father, speaker, and author of *Feeding Baby Green* and *Raising Baby Green*

"*Girl to Girl* is the perfect guide for girls going through the many changes of adolescence! The friendly text, positive attitude, and expert information (from grown-up girls who have 'been there and done that' as well as some medical professionals) provide reassuring advice for young women. I highly recommend this book to my patients who are looking for healthy ways to deal with tween and teen hygiene, practical tips for buying bras, and a whole lot more!"

—Jennifer Shu, MD, Pediatrician, mom, speaker, and co-author of *Food Fights* and *Heading Home with Your Newborn*, and editor of *Baby & Child Health*

"Growing up is never easy, but with today's media pressure on girls to be perfect, it is wonderful to read *Girl to Girl*, a lovely, engaging book for kids going through the transition into puberty. It's a great book for girls to share with their mums, as it will open up dialogue easily and make asking and answering those often embarrassing questions a breeze! The friendly, conversational tone and lively pictures will make it fun to explore the exciting changes involved during puberty."

—Sue Atkins, Parenting coach, speaker, and author of *Parenting Made Easy: How to Raise Happy Children*

"The illustrations, organization, and tone of voice are all pitch perfect for girls entering puberty. Girls will have fun reading this terrific health and hygiene chapter book by themselves, and following up afterwards with questions for mom. *Girl to Girl* will help every girl hold up a thoughtful mirror to her concerns about her changing body, and in a way that should minimize obsessions with body image."

—Joan Jacobs Brumberg, Professor at Cornell University and author of *The Body Project: An Intimate History of American Girls* and *Fasting Girls: The History of Anorexia Nervosa*

"*Girl to Girl* is a must-read for girls and their parents. Filled with practical, sensible, and informative advice from an array of experts and written in a reassuring big sister tone, it's sure to be a great conversation starter for parents who want their daughters to be confident in their changing bodies. Sarah O'Leary Burningham has put together an important resource for girls who will find answers to all of their questions about what's happening with their bodies as they grow up. An added bonus is the wonderful illustrations which help ease discussion about some sensitive topics."

—Sue Scheff, Founder of Parent's Universal Resource Experts, Inc. (P.U.R.E.™) and author of *Wit's End: Advice and Resources for Saving Your Out-of-Control Teen*

"As adult women, we sometimes forget what it feels like to be a young girl entering puberty in a body image–obsessed culture. Sarah O'Leary Burningham has not forgotten. *Girl to Girl* will enable girls to navigate the sometimes treacherous passage into woman-hood while holding on to a healthy sense of self-esteem. I wish *Girl to Girl* had been available for me and my daughters."

—Kate Della-Piana, LCSW, Executive Director, Family Counseling Center

Girl to Girl

Honest Talk About
GROWING UP and Your
CHANGING BODY

By Sarah O'Leary Burningham

Illustrated by Alli Arnold

chronicle books · san francisco

For my sisters: Annie, Katie, and Jennie. Thanks for always being there—
before, during, and after puberty.

And for my daughter, Leigh. I will always be here for you.
—S. B.

Note: Names have been changed to protect girls who shared their stories.

Text © 2014 by Sarah O'Leary Burningham.

Illustrations © 2014 by Alli Arnold.

Library of Congress Cataloging-in-Publication Data

Burningham, Sarah O'Leary.

 Girl to girl : honest talk about growing up and your changing body / by Sarah O'Leary
Burningham ; illustrated by Alli Arnold.

  pages cm

Audience: 8-12.

Audience: Grade 4 to 6.

Includes index.

ISBN 978-1-4521-0242-9 (alk. paper)

1. Girls—Health and hygiene—Juvenile literature. 2. Teenage girls—Health and hygiene—
Juvenile literature. 3. Beauty, Personal—Juvenile literature. 4. Grooming for girls—Juvenile
literature. I. Arnold, Alli, illustrator. II. Title.

RA777.25.B87 2014

613'.04242—dc23

2013008427

Manufactured in China.

MIX
Paper from
responsible sources
FSC® C104723
FSC www.fsc.org

Design by Jennifer Tolo Pierce.

Typeset in Adelle, Galaxie Polaris, Girard Script, and Prater Block One.

The illustrations in this book were rendered in pen, ink, and digital color.

10 9 8 7 6 5 4 3 2 1

Chronicle Books LLC

680 Second Street, San Francisco, California 94107

Chronicle Books—we see things differently. Become part of our community
at www.chroniclekids.com.

Contents

INTRODUCTION
Girl Talk 1

First Things First: Your Body's Time
Is the Right Time 3

CHAPTER ONE
Let's Start at the Top!: Everything from Skin
to Glasses, Hair, and Your Happy Smile 5

CHAPTER TWO
Body Basics: Growth Spurts, Body Odor, Sprouting Hair,
and Other Changes Happening on the Outside 37

CHAPTER THREE
Bust-ed!: Buds, Breasts, and Bras 57

CHAPTER FOUR
Let's Talk, Period: What You Need to Know About
Menstruation 77

CHAPTER FIVE
Be Good to Your Body: All About Healthy Habits 99

CHAPTER SIX
You Are Still You!: Dealing with the Emotional Parts
of Puberty 117

ACKNOWLEDGMENTS
126

INDEX
128

Girl Talk

As the oldest of four girls, I had plenty of girl talk while I was growing up. I was the first of us to develop, which means my sisters came to me with lots of questions. We talked about everything, from shaving our legs to wearing bras. Since then, I've written a few books for girls, and I've had the chance to interview thousands of teens. I've gotten countless questions—and real-life stories—from girls like you about what it's like to grow up. So, while you read this book and go through puberty, think of me as a big sister. I've been there, and I'm going to share everything I know.

I remember the day in fifth grade when I officially learned about puberty. The boys left the classroom with the gym coach, and the girls stayed with our teacher. She drew the shades and turned on an animated video about our bodies. It was hard not to giggle at the cartoon character on the screen, especially when she clutched her stomach and said, "I have cramps!" All of us were laughing nervously. Sure, it looked funny in the movie, but were cramps really going to be that bad? And what about all the other stuff—like wearing deodorant and actually getting my period?

That night, my mom sat me down and asked if I had any questions. I'd had so many while I was sitting in class, but I was nervous—even with my own mom!—and the entire video was jumbled in my brain. My mom told me I would probably have lots of questions during the next few years. And I did! There's no way I could've figured out the answer to every single thing in that one night. With every change, whether it was shaving my armpits or using tampons, I had new questions. And you will, too.

Whether you're feeling ready for puberty or a little unsure of what's happening inside you, this book is here to help you along the way. We'll talk about all the changes you can expect and how to deal with them. Whether you want to know how to find the right bra size or how to deal with acne, I'll help you get to the bottom of things, as well as explore common rumors and myths. I also answer questions from real girls that deal with everything from how to handle sweat stains to whether it's okay to swim when you have your period. Your body is an amazing thing, and understanding how it works will help you be healthy and happy.

I was lucky that my mom was around to answer my questions, and you have people who care about you, too. While you're reading this book and thinking about all the changes you're going through, be sure to talk to your parents or another adult you trust. It might feel embarrassing to talk about your body—it's normal to want to keep some things private—but they're here to help. Even though it might be hard to imagine, every single woman you know has been through what you are going through, from your female teachers to the latest movie star to your mom or stepmom. And men have to go through puberty as well (though it's a little different for them), which means you shouldn't feel embarrassed talking to your dad or stepdad or another trusted adult male. Puberty is part of growing up for everyone.

The most important thing to remember while you're dealing with all these body changes is how amazing you are. Even though I giggled when I watched that video in my fifth-grade class, I remember thinking how impressive it was that my body would just know, on its own, when it was time to start growing up. Think about it. An airplane can't fly itself, and even the fastest computer in the world needs someone to turn it on. But your body is able to figure out exactly what to do and when to do it so you develop into a woman. How cool is that?

So over the next few years, remember to be patient with your body—and yourself. Growing up is an adventure, and that means you'll have some ups *and* some downs. But I'm here to help you get through it all and have fun in the process. Ready? Let's get going!

xxx Sarah

First Things First
Your Body's Time Is the Right Time

Even though puberty seems like it's all about physical changes in your body, it actually starts inside your brain. When you reach a certain age—for most girls, between eight and twelve years old—your brain starts sending out hormone signals to your body that it's time to get ready for puberty. You won't know that these signals are happening—they're part of your normal body function, just like breathing.

Using these hormone signals as instructions, your body starts doing its job—growing. I mean *really* growing. Puberty usually lasts three to four years, and during that time you will become taller and rounder, your breasts will develop, you will start your period, and you will grow pubic hair and hair on the rest of your body. You are a growing machine! It's a lot of work for your body, so your brain keeps the hormones pumping, which is why you might feel emotional during puberty, too.

It's important to remember that you'll start on this puberty journey at the time that's right for your body. Since every girl has a different body, you can't expect to start developing at an exact age or in a certain grade, and you probably won't develop at the same time as your friends or classmates. Some girls start maturing early, while others are "late bloomers." You might start puberty around the same age your mom did, but there's no guarantee. When I started my period, I was almost four years younger than my mom was when she got hers, but my sister started at the same age as my mom. Don't worry if you are at a different stage than your sister or friends. Just like no one else on earth has your same fingerprint, no other girl will have your exact same experience going through puberty. And that's a good thing. You are 100 percent original!

CHAPTER ONE

Let's Start at the Top!

Everything from Skin to Glasses, Hair, and Your Happy Smile

Wash Your Face!

Now that you are going through puberty, you need to start washing your face every single night to keep it clean after a busy day at school or playing softball with friends. Most girls who wash their faces right before bedtime don't need to worry about doing it again in the morning.

Skin care expert Dr. Rosemarie Ingleton, director of Ingleton Dermatology in New York City, says, "the most common mistake that young girls seem to make when dealing with skin care is they wash their faces *too* much. They think that every problem they have on their skin is due to dirt—so they wash and scrub and wash again." Your skin needs some oil to be healthy. Don't strip *all* the oils from it by washing your face too much or being too rough—no harsh scrubbing!

A regular bar of body soap is too harsh for most girls' faces. Instead, Dr. Ingleton recommends using a "gentle soap-free liquid cleanser." You can get effective, inexpensive cleansers at the drugstore. Don't worry about whether it's a name brand. Just make sure the label says "noncomedogenic," which means it won't block your pores. If you have more than a few pimples, talk to a parent about trying an over-the-counter acne cleanser with benzoyl peroxide. Just be careful, since this medication can dry out skin, causing itching and redness. You may want to apply a thin layer of lotion to your face after washing, especially if you have dry skin. (I do.) Again, you want to use noncomedogenic lotion, and there's no need to go overboard. More is *not* better when it comes to your skin, and too much lotion will close your pores and cause break-outs.

Acne = Zits = Pimples = Blemishes = Breaking Out

When we talk about skin care, we have to talk about acne. It comes with the puberty territory. There's no need to freak out about getting pimples or zits—they're just a fact of life. Nearly everyone you know will get a few pimples. But what *is* acne? And what can you do about it?

Dr. Ingleton says that "acne is caused by a combination of three things: excessive oil production by the oil glands, an overgrowth of skin bacteria inside the pores, and clogging of the pores."

Basically, during puberty, your hormones jump-start your oil glands and tell them to start pumping out oil. The oil production is all fine and good, until the extra oil becomes too much for skin to handle and it starts clogging your pores (tiny, nearly microscopic, "holes" in your skin). Mix the extra oil with the dirt and sweat that get into pores during a normal day, and your skin gets irritated. And that's how you get pimples. Acne can also be hereditary, which means it might run in your family. Talk to your parents to see if they had acne problems when they were teenagers.

Noncomedogenic = good for your skin!

Sarah's Tip: No Picking!

It can be tempting to pick at or pop zits. But don't do it! It can spread the bacteria that caused them in the first place, causing even more pimples, and can leave scars.

Pimples come in a few different forms:

Swollen Lesions: These are typical zits, or pimples, which occur when pores become blocked and turn red or fill with pus.

Whiteheads: Whiteheads look like little white dots under the skin. They develop when oil and bacteria get trapped right below the skin's surface.

Blackheads: Blackheads form when oil and bacteria are trapped below the skin's surface. They look black because the bacteria have reacted with oxygen at some point. Even though blackheads look like little specs of dirt, they are deep under your skin, so don't pick them. Just keep washing your face, and the bacteria will slowly work their way out of the pore.

MYTH BUSTER: Oil Is NOT All Bad!

Even though oil can cause acne, it's not all bad. You can't stop your hormones from producing oil, and you don't want to. Oil is a good, natural thing in your skin and hair. It's only a problem when it gets out of control. That's why the #1 thing you can do to treat acne is keep your skin clean. And the best way to do that is to wash your face. Changing your pillowcase regularly and keeping your phone clean helps, too. Think about all the times you dial your BFF or text your mom—if you don't wipe the phone down, all the germs from your fingers and hands just end up on your face!

If you wash your face daily and still get acne that's painful or leaves scars, you might want to see a doctor. If your family doctor thinks you need special skin care, he or she will refer you to a dermatologist, a doctor who specializes in skin conditions. Dermatologists often prescribe special face washes and medicines for serious acne problems. Even if your acne is mild, you might still want to get some acne medication or use a particular kind of face wash. A dermatologist can help figure out the best treatment and products for your skin type.

Carmindy's Top Five Favorite Face Tips

Carmindy, a professional makeup artist, TV personality, creator of her own makeup line, and bestselling author, spends almost every day of her life talking to women and girls about their faces, so she really knows her stuff. And she shared a few of her top skin care tips for you!

✳ Remember to be gentle with your face. You will have it all your life.

✳ Wash your face every single night.

✳ Never pick at a pimple.

✳ No harsh rubbing of your eyes.

✳ When you look in the mirror, don't EVER say anything negative. Instead, find a mirror mantra and focus on something you like about yourself, like "I have a beautiful smile." It will make you feel good.

☆ **GET CONFIDENT**: Ads Don't Matter! ☆

There's a lot of information out in the world, especially in ads and commercials, that might make you feel embarrassed by puberty. The girls in acne commercials are usually humiliated because they have a zit: "Oh, my gosh! A zit, right before the big dance!" But guess what? Everyone gets zits! So when you see or hear something like this, just remind yourself that they're trying to convince you to buy their acne cream.

Although it's not fun to get a pimple or pimples, try not to dwell on it. The more you think about it, the worse you'll feel. And chances are, it's not as noticeable to everyone else as it is to you. Being able to feel a zit on your face makes it automatically seem bigger than it really is. (Especially if it's one of those pimples that kind of hurts!) The good news is that break-outs don't last forever, so try not to make each zit the center of your universe.

Fun in the Sun: Wear Sunscreen!

One of the most important things you can do for your face is to wear sunscreen. And not just when you're at the beach. Get in the habit of applying it every day. Many moisturizers provide some sun protection and are great if you don't feel like putting on an extra layer when you leave the house. Don't be fooled if it's overcast or rainy—you can get sunburned even when it's cloudy out. Sunburns aren't fun, and too much sun exposure can lead to skin cancer.

Use a sunscreen that provides broad spectrum protection from both UVB and the entire UVA spectrum of rays and has an SPF of at least 15. SPF stands for Sun Protection Factor, and a sunscreen marked SPF 15 will give you fifteen times the protection you would have with bare skin. There's no need to get higher than an SPF 30, because higher SPF numbers don't offer any additional protection. Sunscreens come in many different formulas—sprays, lotions, creams, gels, and even wet wipes! If you get acne, look for "oil free" or "noncomedogenic" on the label so your pores don't get clogged. Be sure to put on enough to really cover your skin and read the directions to know how often to reapply it.

Protect Yourself from Skin Cancer

When my sister Annie was a teenager, she would lie out for hours to get tan. Then, when she was in college, she had to have a melanoma (a group of skin cancer cells) removed from her back because of all the time she'd spent tanning. Now she has to be extra careful so she doesn't get skin cancer again.

You don't need to be afraid that you'll get cancer from small amounts of sun exposure. It's fun to be in the sun—swimming, playing soccer, even skiing in the wintertime—and it gives you an important dose of vitamin D. Simply wear sunscreen and cover up with a hat and lightweight clothing to protect your skin when you're outside.

And never, ever, use tanning beds. The rays of light from tanning beds are even more dangerous than the sun because they are concentrated and come from a source close to your skin.

Although fair-skinned people have a higher risk, girls of all skin tones—from fair to olive to dark—can get skin cancer, so you still need to take precautions, no matter what your complexion. Take care of your skin and encourage your friends to protect theirs, too!

Fabulous Freckles

Freckles, little spots on your skin that have extra pigment (or color) can be found all over the body, including the face. They are usually seen on people with light or fair skin and are mostly hereditary, which means they run in your family. You can also get freckles from being in the sun, since the sun's rays can darken the pigment in your skin faster.

There's an old saying that freckles come from the kiss of an angel. Who wouldn't want to be kissed by an angel? People with freckles tend to be more sensitive to the sun, so if you have freckles, take care of them (and the rest of your skin) by wearing sunscreen.

Holy Moley: What Is a Mole?

Moles are similar to freckles. They look like dark spots on your skin and are made up of a tight cluster of pigmented, or colored, skin cells. Moles are usually brown or black, but sometimes they can appear reddish, pink, white, tan, or even bluish. They come in all shapes and sizes, and might be flat or raised, round or irregularly shaped.

Almost every single person on the planet has a mole, and most people develop new moles during childhood. Most moles are harmless—they are often called beauty marks. Healthy moles are usually symmetrical, which means that if you folded the mole in half, the two halves would match up. But if any of your moles change in shape, height, size, or color, you should see a doctor. Pay special attention to any moles that get a lot of sun, like the moles on your arms, neck, face, and legs, because some moles can develop into melanoma, a form of skin cancer.

You don't need to lose sleep worrying about your moles becoming cancerous, but it's something you should be aware of. Take a mental picture of your moles and then, every month or so, do a quick once-over in the shower to see if anything has changed.

Makeup: To Wear or Not to Wear

Wearing makeup is definitely part of growing up for some girls, but nobody *needs* to use it to feel and look beautiful. Some of the most beautiful girls I know go *au naturel*. And it's not just a looks thing—some girls don't like makeup because it feels gunky on their faces or makes them break out.

But say you want to give makeup a try. Chances are, if your mom is anything like mine, you have family rules about when you can start wearing it. Believe it or not, makeup doesn't just go on perfectly. Learning to apply it takes practice, which is another reason you want to wait until the time is right and your parents are okay with you wearing it.

Makeup can be a fun way to express your style, but a good general rule is that less is more. Here's the thing with makeup: It might look light in the package, but on your face, the color can turn out darker and more intense. You don't want your makeup to look like it's wearing you. So start slow and use a light hand.

Using tinted lip balm or clear lip gloss is a good first step. I always loved flavored Lip Smackers (Dr. Pepper was my fave because of the color and the taste). Try to get one that moisturizes and has SPF to protect your lips. Then, when you're old enough, you can try a light mascara or a soft blush.

After you experiment with makeup, you might find that you don't even like wearing it. My sister Jennie loves playing with different looks for different events, while my sister Katie, who used to beg my mom almost every day to let her wear makeup, now prefers being fresh-faced. Either way, keep it light so people can see *you* and not just the makeup you're wearing.

Most makeup is made to stay on all day, which means you have to take some extra steps to remove it at night. Not taking off your makeup can result in clogged pores and acne. Liquid eye-makeup remover or removal wipes make it easy to clean off mascara or eye shadow.

Girl Talk: Am I Too Young to Start Wearing Makeup?

Dear Sarah,
When do you think it's okay to start wearing makeup? I'm almost thirteen, but my mom says I'm too young. When did you start wearing makeup?
Ally

Dear Ally,
I remember feeling the same way when my mom said I wasn't quite old enough to wear makeup. So we struck a deal. I wasn't allowed to wear makeup outside, but my mom would let me play with it when I was at home. I didn't get to do it all the time, but on special nights she gave me permission to try different looks with her makeup, and sometimes she would even do my makeup for me. It was really fun! And it helped me get the hang of applying lip gloss for when I was allowed to wear it. When I talked to Carmindy about this, she said that toenail polish can also be a fun way to try different looks without wearing makeup on your face.

When I was fourteen, my mom let me start wearing colored lip balm and gloss to school, but that was just the age at our house. Talk to your parents about what age they think would be right for you to start putting on makeup or nail polish. Until that time comes, ask your mom how she feels about you playing with some light makeup at home. It's a fun way to prepare for wearing makeup for real and is something you might be able to do together.

Good luck!

XXX Sarah

At Home Spa: Oatmeal Face Mask

Every few months, I treat myself to an oatmeal face mask. Oatmeal is a great natural ingredient that calms and moisturizes skin. You don't need fancy or expensive products to feel great! Plus, you can do this at home. Just be sure to get a parent's go-ahead if you make it using a food processor or blender.

WHAT YOU'LL NEED:

½ cup (40 grams) oatmeal

½ cup (120 milliliters) plain yogurt

2 tablespoons honey

WHAT TO DO:

* If you're using a food processor or blender, grind up the oatmeal to make it a fine powder. If not, you can just skip this step.

* In a small bowl, combine the oatmeal, yogurt, and honey. Mix with a fork until it's a smooth paste. It's going to be thick!

* Pat the mixture onto your clean face, avoiding your eyes. Let it sit for 10 to 15 minutes. It will get cakey and dry.

* Using a damp washcloth, wipe the mask from your face and then rinse over the sink to get the last pieces off.

Voilà! Clean and calm skin.

Smart Mouth

Your skin isn't the only part of your face that needs taking care of. Your mouth sees a lot of action during the day. It helps chew, talk, smile, and laugh. It's a busy body part!

You might remember losing your first baby tooth (plus all the rest after that!), and getting your permanent grown-up teeth. These teeth need to last the rest of your life. If you lose one, there's not another that will grow in. And that means you've got to take care of them.

The most important thing you can do to take care of your teeth is brush them regularly. Brush twice a day—once in the morning when you wake up and again before you go to sleep—for at least two minutes. Try listening to a song or timing yourself to figure out how long two minutes really is . . . it's longer than you think!

Brushing keeps your mouth feeling fresh and your breath smelling good. The bacteria that form cavities and plaque don't smell (or taste) very good. You know how your mouth feels dry and your breath feels thick when you wake up in the morning? The bacteria in your mouth have been going at it all night, coating your teeth, gums, and tongue. A good brushing stops the bacteria in their tracks.

2 x 2 = 2 times a day for 2 minutes each

And, here's another Rule of 2 for you! You should really visit the dentist two times a year (every six months) to get your teeth cleaned and checked out.

Brushing 101

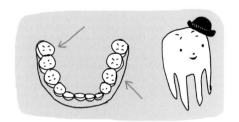

1) Use a small dab of toothpaste, about the size of your pinkie nail.

2) Start in the back of your mouth with your molars and move the toothbrush in small circles around the top and sides of each tooth. Do both top and bottom rows, lightly brushing the gums, too.

3) Next, give your tongue a turn! That way, you're cleaning out your whole mouth, which is good to do since the bacteria on your tongue are what cause bad breath.

4) Rinse your mouth with water (you don't want to swallow toothpaste!). If you want, you can also rinse with mouthwash, which helps kill any extra germs.

Do You Know . . .
the Difference Between Plaque and Tartar?

Plaque is a white, yellow-tinted, or transparent layer of bacteria and other particles that forms on your teeth after you eat and drink. If left alone, it will eventually turn into tartar. Tartar is a hardened, more advanced form of plaque that causes decay. It will literally kill your teeth. Brushing regularly will keep plaque and tartar off your pearly whites.

Keep Cavities Out!

Cavities are teeny tiny holes in the hard enamel of your teeth that are formed by the acids produced by bacteria. Once they are there, they won't go away on their own. You have to have a dentist fill them up, or they grow and eventually, rot out your entire tooth. Ouch! To avoid cavities, start by making sure your toothpaste has fluoride in it. Fluoride is a mineral that fights bacteria and strengthens the enamel coating on the tooth so that the acids produced by the bacteria cannot eat through. Your city might put fluoride in its water (that's how important it is!), but if it doesn't, you can get the fluoride you need from your toothpaste or fluoride rinses.

How to Spot a Cavity: Dr. Joseph Checchio of Genesis Dental in Utah says a warning sign of a cavity is a quick, sharp sting on a tooth when you eat something sugary or a jolt of pain when you take a bite of hot food or drink something cold. If you feel any tooth pain, get your dentist to check it out right away.

Brush Up! Finding the Right Toothbrush

Traditional Toothbrushes: Most dentists recommend using toothbrushes with soft bristles. The package label will tell you if a toothbrush is "soft," "medium," or "hard." The soft types are less likely to scrape and damage your gums when you brush. Remember, you want to brush firmly, but you don't need to push hard to make a difference.

Electric Toothbrushes: An electric toothbrush rotates the head in circles so you don't have to!

It's a good idea to get a new toothbrush (or a new head for your electric brush) about every three months, because after a while, the bristles get worn down and aren't as effective.

Flossing

Brushing gets the bacteria from the tops and sides of your teeth and gums, but what about all those tiny spaces in between your teeth? That's where dental floss comes in. Flossing is a good habit to get into now, since you probably have most of your permanent teeth. You need to floss once a day to keep your gums healthy.

Flossing 101

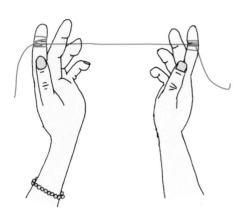

1) Pull out a new piece of floss thread (about the length from your wrist to your elbow) every time you floss. Wrap one end of the floss a few times around a finger on each hand, leaving 2 to 3 inches (about 5 to 7 centimeters) in between. Your fingers will hold the floss tight like a violin string. Most people like to use the index or middle fingers for this, but experiment to see what works best for you. (You can also buy floss picks. These look like plastic forks with two tongs and floss in between, already pulled taut for you.)

2) Ease the tight section of the floss between two teeth (keeping one finger in back of the teeth and one finger in front), and wrap the floss around a tooth. Gently slide the floss up and down in a sawing motion. Use the edge of the floss to pull any plaque (gunky clear or white stuff) away from each tooth near the gums. Remember to be gentle! Flossing too hard will make your gums bleed.

3) To get the most out of your floss, rinse it off in the sink every few teeth. When you're done, rinse your mouth out and throw away the floss.

While I'm flossing at night, I like to think about my favorite parts of the day. It's like keeping a mental journal, and it prevents flossing from getting boring.

☆ **GET CONFIDENT**: Whiter Isn't Always Better ☆

Have you noticed all the ads and commercials for products that are supposed to make your teeth whiter? The truth is, your teeth aren't supposed to be as white as snow. But by making you unhappy with your appearance, these companies get you to buy their products, and that means they make more money.

You should always be careful before trying anything that changes your appearance, and that includes tooth whiteners. Some treatments can weaken the enamel on your teeth (which leads to cavities!) and even damage your gums.

To keep your teeth's natural whiteness, avoid foods and drinks that are very acidic or high in sugar, like soda, since they can actually stain the enamel, making your teeth appear slightly yellow, brown, or just dull.

I understand wanting to have whiter teeth, but make sure you don't go overboard. Having teeth that glow in the dark can look almost alien, and you still want to look like yourself!

A Little Lip

Your teeth aren't the only part of your mouth that you need to think about. Your lips also need some TLC—dry air, both hot and cold, can cause them to chap and peel. If you get chapped lips, apply some lip balm or petroleum jelly (like Vaseline) to keep them from cracking and hurting. You can reapply until your lips heal. Usually your body does a fine job of keeping your lips as moist as they need to be, so you don't always need lip balm, but it's not a bad idea to wear a version with SPF when you're outside. Your lips get sunburned just like the rest of you!

Brace Yourself: All About Braces

Straight teeth look nice, but that's not the only reason for braces. Having your teeth aligned properly, so the top teeth meet the bottom teeth in just the right way, is important for chewing, talking, and avoiding dental problems (like tooth decay) when you're older. Not all kids who need braces get them. The truth is, your parents will have to pay quite a bit of money for them. If you need braces and are fortunate enough to be able to have them, remember that the process doesn't take forever. They'll be off sooner than you think. In the meantime, just think about the hard work they are doing: Every day, your teeth are moving a microscopic amount. When your braces are off, your teeth will be straight, you'll have a good bite, and you'll be able to talk, chew, and smile more easily than before.

There are several different kinds of braces. The traditional metal kind are made up of small metal brackets that are glued to the front of each tooth and connected by a wire. Tiny rubber bands (which come in a bunch of different colors!) help hold the wire in place. Over time, the wire pulls your teeth

straight and into position for a good, healthy bite. An orthodontist will usually do a checkup about once a month to make sure your braces are still in line and to adjust, or "tighten," them. Your teeth might ache for a few days right after an orthodontist visit because they move the most when the wire is at its tightest.

A lot of orthodontists also offer "invisible" braces, but these are only for certain types of mouths, depending on what kind of straightening and realigning you need. Invisible-style braces aren't actually invisible. They are clear, plastic molds of your teeth that cup around each row, one for the top set of teeth, another for the bottom. You wear the "braces" all day, every day, except when you are eating, brushing, and flossing. Your orthodontist may also be able to offer you ceramic brackets that blend in with your tooth color better or braces that attach behind your teeth instead of on the front. Your dentist or orthodontist will be able to tell you which kinds of braces are best for your mouth.

When I got my braces off, I had to wear a retainer for another year, to keep my teeth in place. Your braces have done a lot of work, and the retainer prevents your teeth from moving back. A retainer is a piece of plastic formed to the top of your mouth with a wire that wraps around the front of your teeth. How long you wear a retainer, and whether you even need one, depends on your teeth, but it's pretty standard to wear one for a while after having braces.

> It's easy to keep your retainer clean by brushing it with a toothbrush and toothpaste. Be sure to brush it when you brush your teeth every morning and night.

The most important thing you can do to take care of your teeth while wearing braces is to brush and floss at least twice a day. (You should floss more than usual while you have on braces.) Good dental hygiene is always important, but it's even more important when you have braces. You'll be happy you did when you get those braces off and your teeth are straight and healthy!

Girl Talk: Will Braces Leave Spots on My Teeth?

Dear Sarah,
My orthodontist says I have to wear braces for two years, and I heard that if you don't brush your teeth a lot when you have braces, the rest of your teeth get yellow, and when you get the braces off, there are white spots on them from where the braces were. Can this really happen?
    Jami

Dear Jami,
It's true that if you don't take care of your teeth, sugary or acidic foods (think candy bars or soda) will stain the enamel, making the exposed areas darker and leaving lighter spots in the places where the metal brackets of your braces were attached. To make sure this doesn't happen, brush and floss twice a day, and really spend time with the floss to clean out the spots around the metal brackets.

xxx Sarah

Sarah's Tip: Braces Before and After

Since braces don't move your teeth overnight, you won't be able to see a difference from day to day. So, to remind yourself why you have the braces in the first place, take a picture of yourself before you get them on. Over the months, look back at the pictures. After a while, you will start to see tiny changes. It's nice to see that your braces are actually working!

BEFORE   AFTER

Eye See You: Glasses and Contacts

I got my first pair of glasses in fourth grade. I didn't realize I needed them until one day at school I asked my teacher if she could write something a little bigger on the chalkboard because her writing was too small for me to read. It turned out that her writing wasn't too small at all, but that my vision was changing, and suddenly I couldn't read everything on the chalkboard. I needed glasses! If you ever have a hard time seeing things, whether far away like a movie screen or close like a book, it's worth getting an eye test to check your vision.

If You're Nearsighted: You see things better when they're close up. But your eyes don't focus correctly on faraway objects, so they look blurry.

If You're Farsighted: You see things better when they're far away. Your eyes can't focus properly on objects that are up close, like words in a book.

My mom and I went to the eye doctor, and sure enough, I was nearsighted. We ordered dark purple, almost black, frames (so chic!) and picked them up a few days later. When I put my glasses on for the first time, suddenly there were all these things I'd never noticed before! I saw little tiny flowers on a tree and a stoplight I'd never really paid attention to. I didn't realize what a difference it could make to see well.

Even though I really liked my glasses, I was worried that kids in my class would call me "four eyes" or some other mean name. But nobody even noticed, and I almost wished they had at least said something about my cute new look.

When I was fifteen, I got contacts. Most doctors recommend that you wait until you are a teenager to get contacts because they require a lot of cleaning, and they are fragile. Not to mention, it takes a few weeks to get the hang of putting them in! It's a weird sensation to poke little pieces of plastic into your eyes on purpose.

There are some benefits to wearing contacts. For me, they were better for playing sports and doing things outdoors because I didn't have to worry about breaking my glasses, and I didn't have the edges of the frames of my glasses to limit my vision. For a few years, I wore my contacts almost every day. But then I decided to go back to my cute purple glasses—they just added more to my look! I still wear my glasses more than contacts, not just because they are more comfortable, but because they are part of my style!

Fab Frames 101

Pick a style of glasses that's as stylish as you!

Cat Eye: These frames slant upward near the temples, kind of like a cat's eyes, and were very popular in the '50s.

Round: Round glasses were worn by a lot of '60s rockers, and by Harry Potter.

Big Plastic Frames: This style is kind of geek chic. Back in the day, they used to be a little dorky, but now they're totally cool among the college kids I see in New York.

Wire: Wire frames are more delicate than plastic frames, and are usually lighter, so they aren't as heavy on the bridge of your nose. They can make you look smart and hip.

Rimless: These glasses don't have plastic or wire around the lenses and they give off a creative feel.

Even if you don't need glasses to correct your vision, wearing polarized sunglasses when you're outside can protect your eyes from the sun!

Pierced Ears or Not?

If we move over from your eyes, we come to . . . your ears! I couldn't wait to get my ears pierced, but my sisters and I weren't allowed to get our ears pierced until our twelfth birthdays. There's no right or wrong age to get your ears pierced. It just depends on your family rules.

If you do get your ears pierced, make sure that the holes heal correctly and don't get infected. Keep the starter earrings in your ears for at least a month, and during that time, put some rubbing alcohol on a cotton ball or cotton swab and rub it on the front and back of your piercing twice a day, to keep the hole disinfected. You should also twirl your starter earrings a few times a day while they are in your ears.

If your pierced ears get infected, keep the holes clean with disinfectant and antibiotic ointment. Talk to your doctor if the infection doesn't go away after a few days, if it seems to spread, or if you develop a fever.

One of my friend's pierced ears were always inflamed. The doctor told her that she was allergic to metal, so she let her holes grow back in. I didn't even notice, until one day, when we were shopping together, I showed her some earrings that I thought would be cute on her. She showed me she didn't have any holes and said she thought everyone had noticed. But she was the only one! It just goes to show you, pierced ears are fun but not necessary. Do what's right for you. If you don't pierce your ears, you can always choose to wear cuffs, stick-on, or clip-on earrings.

NEVER pierce your own ears! One of my sisters attempted piercing at home, and the hole ended up infected and deformed. Piercing is something you need a professional for. You're poking a hole in your body—technically, that's surgery!

Can You Hear Me Now?

The outsides of your ears aren't the only parts that need care. Your eardrums matter, too. It's important to protect your hearing, so when you're using headphones or earbuds, don't have the music turned up too loud. This is especially

important with earbuds, since they fit right inside your ear and force your eardrum to absorb most of the sound.

A good rule of thumb when using any kind of headphones is to keep the volume level at 60 percent of maximum. That way, you'll be able to hear your tunes but won't do any permanent damage to your hearing. Listening to music for long periods of time can be unhealthy, too, so always be sure to give your ears a rest after listening to music for a while.

Hair Care

We've finally reached the top of your head, and what do we find there? Your hair! Long hair, short hair, curly hair, straight hair, wavy hair, kinky hair, frizzy hair, thick hair, fine hair. There are so many different textures of hair, not to mention the colors! Blond, red, brown, black . . . these are the general words that describe hair color, but what about all the combinations? Golden blond, strawberry blond, auburn, chestnut brown, deep black. Between your hair texture and color, you've got a combination that was created by your genes just for you.

Caring for your hair is a lot like caring for your skin. You want to keep it clean, but you don't want to wash it too much and strip its natural oils, drying it out. What's the best way to keep your hair healthy? Regular haircuts every few months to trim the ends, regular washing, and for some girls, conditioning, are all important. But most girls don't need to wash their hair every single day, unless it's dirty or overly oily.

Hair Care 101

Here are some basic hair-washing tips:

* You only need a nickel-size drop of shampoo. Just work it into a lather in your palms and then rub it into your hair.

* There's no need to repeat! The label on your shampoo might say that you should wash, rinse, and repeat, but one shampoo is plenty to get your hair and scalp clean.

* Don't scratch your scalp. A little massage is fine, but remember, your scalp is sensitive, and you need to be gentle with it.

* If your hair ends up in knots after a shower or you have really curly hair, you might want to try conditioner or detangler.

Brush Happy

When you first get out of the shower, gently pull a wide-toothed comb through your hair to avoid tangles. If you pull too hard, you can break your hair. If you have curly hair, you can use your fingers to gently comb through your curls and then let them go!

Don't brush or comb your hair too much—brushing a lot can activate the glands in your scalp and make your hair oily. It can also break the ends of your hair, causing split ends. If you are going to brush your hair, wait until it's dry. Girls with curly hair might find it's best to avoid brushes altogether. Brushing curly hair can damage it and make it frizzy.

At Home Spa:
Avocado Conditioning Treatment

Avocados have a lot of wonderful natural fats and essential oils, which make them yummy to eat and also great for your hair. That's right! You can use avocados at home to make a special conditioning mask for healthy, shiny hair. Just be sure you have permission and apply the mask in the shower to avoid making a mess.

WHAT YOU'LL NEED:

1 ripe avocado

2 tablespoons olive oil

1 tablespoon honey

WHAT TO DO:

✳ Cut the avocado, remove the pit, and peel away the skin. (Be sure to follow house rules for using knives and ask for help if you haven't done this before.) Then, mash the insides of the avocado in a bowl.

✳ Add the oil and honey, mashing and mixing until everything is creamy smooth.

✳ Take the mixture into the shower or bathtub (just to make sure it doesn't get everywhere as you apply it) and rub it all over your hair, from the scalp to the ends. Read a book and relax for 15 to 20 minutes while you wait for it to soak in.

✳ Rinse thoroughly with shampoo and warm water.

What to do if your hair is . . .	Dry	Oily
Symptoms	If your hair has lots of static energy, gets frizzy, or feels brittle, it's probably dry. If your hair is dry, your scalp might be dry, too, and feel itchy or tight.	Oily hair feels slick and might look greasy, even just a few hours after washing. But believe it or not, your hair isn't what's oily. It's your scalp!
Treatments	Cutting back on how often you wash your hair can help you keep the natural moisture in your scalp and hair. You can also try a shampoo and conditioner made especially for dry hair. These products can help add essential oils back into your strands.	The best thing you can do for oily hair is to keep it clean. You might try a "clarifying" shampoo made for oily hair. Since conditioner basically adds oils to your hair, don't use it on your scalp (hello, oil overload!). Just apply it to the ends—or you might want to skip it all together. Keep in mind that gel or hairspray might add to the oiliness, too.

Sarah's Tip: Stop Static Hair Cling

Sometimes, when you pull a sweatshirt over your hair or it's really dry outside, your hair picks up static electricity and seems to stand straight up and out! If this happens to you, rub a dryer sheet gently over your hair. It takes out the static cling, and your hair will lie flat. How cool is that? Just be sure you aren't allergic to dryer sheets before trying this one!

Natural Hair: Rock What You've Got

The key to having healthy hair is appreciating it and working with what you've got. It's fun to use hair dryers, curling irons, and flat irons sometimes—I have stick-straight hair, and I like to get a little curl every once in a while. But treating your hair with too many products or tools will damage it, so you don't want to use them every day. The best way to have healthy, natural hair is to let it be!

Overheating with a hair dryer, curling iron, or flat iron often causes split ends. A split end is a piece of hair that splits or peels at the bottom. Conditioning can help prevent split ends from forming, but the only way to get rid of them is to cut them off. Regular haircuts keep your ends in tip-top shape!

A Girl Who's Been There:
Don't Worry About Oily Hair

"My hair was oily as a teenager. Actually, I felt like everything about me was oily—my skin, my sweat, my hair. But I couldn't stop touching my hair, and I was constantly pulling it back and brushing it, and then I would touch my face, which probably made my acne worse. The thing is, my hair felt oilier than it looked. I should've just left it alone. No one notices your oily hair but you!"
—Erika

Dealing with Dandruff

Dandruff is a common skin condition in which the skin on your scalp sheds more frequently and in larger pieces than normal. If you have dandruff, you might see white, oily flakes of skin in your hair or on your shoulders. Your scalp will probably feel tight, dry, and itchy. It's normal to see a few flakes in your hair every once in a while, but if the flakes are noticeable on a day-to-day basis, you will want to take action.

If you have dandruff, first try washing your hair normally. If that doesn't help, you might need an over-the-counter medicated shampoo. That should help most cases, but if not, a doctor can give you something stronger or check for other skin conditions that might require more care.

Dandruff isn't something to be embarrassed about. It's easy to take care of, and most people get it at some point.

Girl Talk: Help! Chlorine Turned My Hair Green!

Dear Sarah,
I have blond hair, and I'm on the swim team at my school. Last year, the ends of my hair turned green from the pool. How can I keep that from happening again?
    Caitlin

Dear Caitlin,
Swim team is such a fun way to get exercise and make friends. But it's not fun when your hair changes color! Your hair absorbs a small amount of the chemicals and minerals in the swimming pool water every time it gets wet. After a while, these minerals build up and give your hair a greenish tint. It's more likely to happen to lighter hair, but even darker hair can turn green. There are some easy steps you can follow to make sure it doesn't happen again this year.

Wear a swimming cap when you go in the pool, which can keep your hair from drying out. It also helps if you wet your hair in the shower first—hair that's already wet is less likely to soak up the mineral-filled water from the pool. Be sure to rinse off with fresh water after you get out of the pool, too. There are also special shampoos for swimmers, designed to help combat the problem. Swim on!

xxx Sarah

Lice

Dandruff isn't the only thing you might be worried about when it comes to your scalp. Head lice are tiny insects that live on the scalp. These nearly microscopic bugs bite your skin, make your scalp itch, and lay eggs, which hatch into more lice and make things worse!

It's incredibly common to get head lice at least once in your life, which means it might happen to you. If your scalp feels itchy or if lice are going around at school, have an adult or nurse check your scalp. If you do get lice, you can buy a special shampoo that kills the bugs. You'll also want to wash your clothes, sheets, and anything else that you've been using.

> Be smart about protecting yourself from lice by not sharing hats, brushes, combs, barrettes, or anything else that is in direct contact with someone else's hair. You don't want to be paranoid, because lice aren't the end of the world, but it never hurts to play it safe.

The Best Beauty Secret: Smile Big and Think Happy Thoughts

Every once in a while, you will probably have a day when you are stressed about how you look. Maybe you are too focused on a zit or you feel like your hair doesn't look quite right. Maybe you just got your braces tightened, and feeling them is making you self-conscious. (I always hated that dull ache after getting my braces tightened. It made me think about them more than usual.) No matter what is making you think about your appearance, remember that you are focused on the negatives more than anyone else. Instead of letting small things ruin your day, put a smile on your face and turn your focus to something positive. Everyone will notice your shining, happy smile and not the little things that you are worried about. And wearing a smile will make you happier, too! There are scientific studies that prove your brain takes cues from your facial expressions. Really! So the next time you want to feel and look confident, think about something that makes you happy and put a smile on your face. Your brain should follow suit.

CHAPTER TWO

Body Basics

Growth Spurts, Body Odor, Sprouting Hair, and Other Changes Happening on the Outside

Remember those hormones we talked about at the beginning of the book—the chemicals that start all the changes that come with puberty? Well, even as those hormones are working on the inside, they are changing things on the outside. During puberty, you'll notice a lot of differences in your body and how you look. You'll even smell different!

As you get older, you'll need to learn new ways to keep clean and smell good so you feel your best. You'll also need to be patient. I know a lot of girls who want to be taller or shorter, or have bigger feet (so they can wear their older sister's shoes!) or longer fingers (so they can reach more keys on the piano!). Taking care of your body is also about loving your body. It's important to be nice to yourself as you grow up and not to decide that one height or size is the "right" one. You are meant to be just the way you are.

What Is a Growth Spurt?

A growth spurt is when your body grows anywhere from a couple of inches to a foot (or about 5 to 30 centimeters)—or even more!—in a short period of time. That's why it's called a spurt—the growth is fast, and someone who doesn't see you every day might even say that you "grew overnight!"

I didn't realize I was going through a growth spurt until suddenly my shorts were all too short and I was assigned to stand in the back row of my class picture because I was taller than almost everyone—even the boys! For the next few years, I was one of the tallest in my class. But by the time I started middle school, everyone had seemed to catch up with me.

Not all girls get tall early; some may grow just an inch or two (or several centimeters). Your parents' height will give you a general idea of how tall you might be, but your combination of genes is different from everyone else's—even your parents'—and that means there's no way to predict exactly how tall you'll get. It's up to your body to get you there.

Growth spurts aren't just about getting taller, either. During puberty, you start developing a more womanly

body—your hips will get a little wider, and your butt and thighs might get rounder. Your breasts will also get bigger (and we'll talk more about that in chapter three). You will gain some weight in your entire body as you fill out. Some girls get tall and then round out, while others round out first and then get a little taller. Your body will grow in the order that's best for you.

Squeaky Clean

When you were younger, your parents probably used to give you a bath a few times a week. You probably didn't need one every day (unless you got really dirty!), because your body doesn't sweat as much when you are a kid.

But during puberty, your sweat glands swell and grow (here we go with the growing again!), which causes you to start perspiring or sweating. Sweat, when it mingles with normal bacteria on your skin, starts to smell. And, boy, does it smell! When you get really sweaty and don't clean off, you'll notice that your body starts to have a "ripe" or pungent smell. That's body odor (or BO for short). BO isn't bad—we all smell when we sweat a lot—but now that you are sweating and have body odor, you will need to take a bath or shower more often.

How often you need to bathe depends on how much you sweat, but it's a good rule of thumb to plan a bath or shower every day or, at the very least, every other day. If you play softball or take dance or do anything else that's really active, you might need to shower more frequently.

Wearing Deodorant

Another good habit that will keep you smelling fresh is wearing deodorant. You can buy it as a gel, liquid roll-on, or solid. The gel and liquid varieties take a little longer to feel dry under your arms and are usually clear. The solid kind usually looks slightly white or powdery once it's on your skin. There are some great natural and organic brands of deodorant that are good for sensitive skin— and for the planet! Different girls like different kinds, so try them out to see which one feels the best for you.

Sarah's Tip: Do Away with Deodorant Streaks

I always smear deodorant on my shirts when I am getting dressed. Even when I am super careful, it still happens. I can't help it!

If you get deodorant on your clothes, like me, just get a soft, dry washcloth and rub it gently on the white spot. The fabric of the washcloth will pick up the particles of deodorant off your clothes, magically erasing them!

Deodorant goes only under your arms, in your armpits. One girl I know thought it was supposed to go everywhere (it does smell nice, after all!), and she was rubbing it up and down her legs when her mom walked into the bathroom and told her it was only for your armpits. She was embarrassed—but, after all, if no one shows you where something is supposed to go, how would you know?

Most people put on deodorant after they get out of the shower (you can reapply after gym class or playing sports, if you want), and one to three swipes under your arms should last the whole day. There's no need to load it on. Remember, sweating isn't bad—it's the way your body cools itself off, like its own air-conditioning system.

DEODORANT OR ANTIPERSPIRANT?

Deodorant and antiperspirant are both designed to keep you from smelling bad, but they are slightly different. Antiperspirant prevents your pores from sweating or perspiring in the first place, so you don't start to smell. That's why it's called ANTIperspirant. Deodorant, on the other hand, doesn't stop you from sweating; it just tries to eliminate the sweaty smell. Many doctors think that deodorant is healthier than antiperspirant. Sweating is a natural way for your body to cool off and release toxins, so you don't want to block sweat. If you can choose between the two, go for the deodorant.

Girl Talk:
How to Handle Sweat Stains

Dear Sarah,
My armpits are really sweaty, and sometimes you can see wetness through my shirt. It's so embarrassing, and I don't want to lift my arms up. What can I do?
    Madison

Dear Madison,
Don't worry! People probably aren't noticing your sweat like you are. After all, you can feel it, so you are much more aware of it. If you are still worried, try to wear looser shirts made of natural fabrics like cotton, which help your armpits "breathe" more easily. Tighter clothes can trap in sweat and can make your armpits feel sticky. Check the tag or label on your clothing to see if it's 100 percent cotton. Try to steer clear of spandex and polyester blends, especially when it's hot.
    You can also keep a small, travel-size antiperspirant in your bag for really hot and humid days. Most important, remember that you are thinking about your sweat more than anyone else is. Try not to focus on it. Sweating shouldn't ruin your day!

xxx Sarah

Body Hair

Getting older means getting hairier. During puberty, you will grow hair in your armpits, on your legs, and even in your pubic or crotch area. (We'll talk more about pubic hair in chapter four.)

In many cultures, women shave their underarms and legs, but it's not something that you have to do. First, talk to your parents about your family traditions to figure out what's best for you.

A Girl Who's Been There:
You Don't Have to Shave

"I don't like shaving. I started when I was a preteen and then, as a teenager, decided I didn't want to do it anymore. Now I just let my hair grow naturally. Women shouldn't have to shave if they don't want to. It's a personal choice."
—Brianna

Girl Talk:
Why Won't My Mom Let Me Shave?

Dear Sarah,

I really want to shave my legs because they are so hairy and the hair is so dark, but my mom won't let me. All of my friends shave, and I feel like such an outcast. I know I shouldn't want to shave just because everyone else is, but I want to anyway. My sister shaves, and she's only a year older than me. How can I convince my mom to let me shave?

    Isabel

Dear Isabel,

The first thing you need to do is figure out why your mom doesn't want you to shave. Since shaving is an ongoing process, once you start, you'll probably be shaving regularly. Maybe your mom doesn't think you're ready to handle it yet. Or maybe she has another reason. You need to talk to her to figure out where she's coming from. Listen to her reasons and share how you're feeling.

    Once you've both heard each other out, you can work together to decide on a shaving time line that will work for you *and* your mom. Remember, your mom loves you, and together, the two of you can work through anything!

XXX Sarah

The Three Shaving Essentials

Keep these in the bathroom for every time you shave.

1) **A Razor:** A lot of razors are decked out with bells and whistles, like pivoting heads (the head is the part with the actual razor blades), padded handles, and "lubricating" strips. There are also razors that boast three or four or five blades. These special features aren't bad, but they aren't necessary either.

A disposable razor is meant to be thrown away after the blade gets dull. With a refillable razor, you just throw away the head and replace it with a new blade cartridge. Most refillable razors come with a few cartridges to get you started, and you can buy new ones as you need them.

2) **Shaving Cream, Gel, or Soap:** You definitely want to have foamy lather on your legs before you shave. Shaving cream or gel is nice to use, but it's not essential—lathered soap will get the job done, too. And don't think you have to get the shaving cream that says it's for women. The men's shaving cream is exactly the same stuff!

3) **Lotion or Moisturizer:** Freshly shaved legs might feel dry and itchy. Rubbing some lotion on them after your shower or bath can help stop that feeling. It's like giving your skin a drink of water.

RAZOR SAFETY: Always handle your razor with care! Only grip the handle and keep your hand steady so you don't drop it. If you need to change the blades on your refillable razor, do it before you get in the shower, since they can be slippery when wet. You know how you are careful when you work with scissors? Razors are just as sharp, if not sharper, so you want to be alert when you are dealing with one.

When it comes to shaving, you just need to make sure that the blades on your razor are clean and sharp. Dull blades can lead to cuts, and dirty blades can lead to infections. You should also be sure your razor doesn't have any nicks or dents—these will catch against your skin as you shave and can cut and chafe you. A smooth razor is much safer and easier on your skin.

Sarah's Tip: Sit Down for Your First Shave

If you are shaving for the first time, it's a good idea to try it sitting down, either inside the bathtub or on the edge. Sitting down will help you keep your balance and focus. As you get more practice, you can begin to shave standing up in the shower.

If you're nervous about shaving alone the first time, ask your mom, your older sister, or a friend who knows how to shave already to help you out. You don't have to invite them into the bathroom while you shower—just sit on the edge of the bathtub with your pant legs rolled up over your knee. This way, you can have some company while you get the hang of shaving.

Shaving 101: Legs

Now that you've got the equipment you need, you're ready to start! While you shave, do not push down on the razor; just let it glide over your skin. And don't shave an area more than once, which can irritate and nick the skin. Remember, take your time— there's no rush.

If you nick or cut yourself, which happens a lot when you are just starting to shave, wash the cut with soap and cold water, then dry it off and put an adhesive bandage on it when you get out of the tub. If the cut is bleeding a lot, show an adult immediately.

1) **Soften Up and Lather Up:** Let your skin and leg hair get wet with warm water for a minute or so. Moist skin is softer and will keep the nicks and cuts to a minimum. Next, apply shaving cream, gel, or soap all over the part you're going to shave. Never rub a razor on dry or bare skin.

2) **Calves and Thighs:** These are easiest, so shave them first! Once you're lathered up, start with the razor above your ankle bones. Slowly pull it up along the skin to just below your knee in one long, smooth stroke. After a few strokes, rinse off your razor blade in the tub or run it under the faucet.

Many girls don't shave their thighs because they are often covered by clothing, and the hair is usually finer. If you do shave your thighs, start at the point above your knee and slowly move the razor in straight lines from the top of your knee to the top of your leg.

3) **Ankles:** Maneuver carefully around your ankles, since they are bonier and have more "edges." If you are standing in the shower, bend over at the waist or place your foot on a ledge (be careful, as showers can get slippery!), so you can get closer to your ankle and see what's going on. Move the razor in short, precise strokes around the ankle bones and NEVER drag the blade over any bones. That will definitely end with some cuts.

4) Knees: Your knees are knobby just like your ankles, so they require a little extra care, too. When you shave the front of your knee, bend your leg so it forms the shape of a mountain with the knee as the peak. Pull the razor in short movements to the near top of the peak and do the same on the other side. To shave the backs of your knees, straighten your leg so the skin is taut—you don't want folds of skin to get caught in the razor.

When you are done shaving, give your legs a rinse with cool water. Then pat them dry with a towel. If they feel sensitive, apply a thin layer of lotion to keep the skin moisturized. And voilà! You have shaved your legs!

Sarah's Tip: Don't Be a Slave to Shaving!

If you decide to shave (and not everyone does), remember that you don't need to do it every day. Your skin will get dry and irritated if you shave too often. How often you need to shave and how often you need to change your razor will depend on your body, since everyone's hair grows at different rates, but as a general rule, shaving every few days or even once a week should be plenty. You'll be able to feel when you get prickly, and that will be a sign that it's time for another shave.

Hair Removal Creams: An alternative to shaving is using a hair removal, or depilatory, cream, which dissolves hair so that it can be rinsed or wiped off. You may have seen these creams at the drugstore near the shaving section. The thing is, depilatories are made with harsh chemicals, and they can irritate sensitive skin. They usually smell really strong, too. Girls with allergies should definitely stay away from them. Be sure you talk to a parent or doctor before you try one, or consider just sticking with shaving, which is what I do. Why rub chemicals on your skin if you don't need to?

Shaving 101: Armpits

Start with the razor at the top of your armpit. Pull it downward in soft, straight strokes. Since armpit hair tends to grow in many different directions, you can also start at the bottom of your armpit and pull the razor up. Use a few different strokes to get all the hair, and rinse the razor blade between armpits to remove any trapped hairs.

A Girl Who's Been There: Armpit Hair Angst!

"Armpit hair. Argh! One day, I was doing my hair in the bathroom, wearing a tank top, and my mom walked in and saw my underarms and said, 'Honey! You have grown some armpit hair.' My dad teased me about it, and it was so horrifying that it's still seared into my memory. Now, I know he wasn't trying to be mean, he was just joking with me, but it was a big deal to me at the time! I should've teased him right back. His armpits are way hairier than mine were!"
—Addison

Razor Burn Rash

If you shave too harshly, use a dull razor, or shave an area that's very sensitive, you can get razor burn—a rash of tiny red bumps on your skin. It can be itchy and irritating, but it won't last forever. Here's how to help it heal:

✳ Take a break and wait for the rash to go away before you shave again. Remember, your skin is alive, and even though it seems tough, it's actually pretty delicate.

✳ Keep the area clean and don't scratch the rash.

✳ Apply unscented lotion or Vaseline in a thin coat over the irritated skin to keep it moisturized and to help it heal.

✳ When you start shaving again, soften the skin with water and use shaving cream, shaving gel, or soap to lubricate the area. You also want to use a new, clean razor and be very gentle.

MYTH BUSTER: Shaving Won't Make Your Hair Grow Back Darker or Thicker

It's a common myth that shaving will make hair on your legs or underarms grow back darker or thicker. Shaving doesn't change your hair at all. Each piece of hair grows out of a follicle that is underneath your skin. When you shave, you are just cutting off the hair. The hair follicle, where the hair grows, stays exactly the same, which means the amount of hair you grow after you shave is exactly the same as before.

If your hair feels thicker after you shave, it's just because the end of the hair is blunt from being shaved. New hair can also look darker since it's fresh and seen against your bare skin, but the color won't change from shaving.

Ingrown Hairs

Using a dull razor can lead to ingrown hairs, which is when the hair gets stuck beneath the surface of the skin and grows back in on itself, causing an infection or bump. If you get an ingrown hair, exfoliate or scrub the area lightly to help remove dead skin cells and bacteria that could be blocking the pore. Regular sugar is a natural exfoliant! Sprinkle a teaspoon of it on the affected area, rinse with soap and water, and dab a zit cream on the spot to help it heal.

Nail Care 101

Since you often shake hands when you meet someone for the first time, it's nice to have clean, well-maintained fingernails. Here are three easy steps to keeping your fingernails tidy:

1) **Scrub Them Down:** Clean dirt out from under the nails with a small scrub brush (they make them just for nails!), soap, and water.

2) **Keep Them Trimmed:** Your nails grow slowly, but you'll still need to cut them about every other week. Position the clippers close to the skin—don't catch any skin between the blades, though. The best way to shape your nails is to cut them straight across. Then smooth and slightly round the edges with a nail file or emery board. Sawing the file back and forth can weaken your nails, so just rub it in one direction. Don't cut or file the edges down below where the skin and cuticle grow; that will give you ingrown nails. And always keep your clippers clean!

3) **Don't Cut the Cuticles!** The cuticle is the strip of skin at the base of your nail. It's an important barrier that protects your nails from germs and infection. If your cuticles start looking scraggly, soak your hands in warm water and then use an orange stick (a long wooden stick with flat ends) to gently push the cuticle down toward the knuckle on each nail. Or apply some cuticle cream!

At Home Spa: Playing with Polish

Nail polish can be a fun way to express your style. Just make sure your parents say it's okay to paint your fingernails or toenails. Do the painting in your bathroom, so that if the polish spills, it won't stain any furniture or the rug. Nail polish is a beast to get out of fabric!

WHAT YOU'LL NEED:

Nail polish—experiment with a fun color!

Rag or towel to put under your hand or foot when you're polishing

Acetone-free nail polish remover

A few cotton balls or cotton swabs

Get Creative with Your Polish Designs!

Try polka dots in different colors by dotting the tip of the polish brush in a few spots on each nail. You can also do stripes, diamond shapes, or even smiley faces!

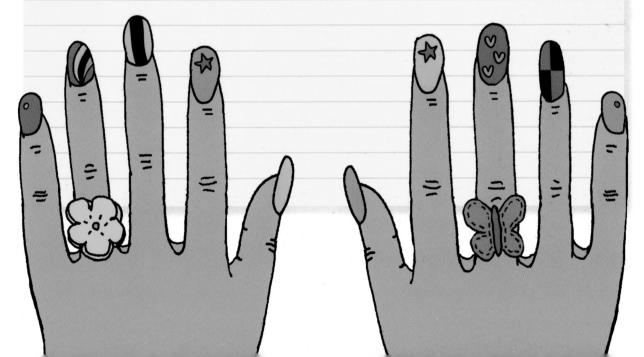

Healthy Hands and Feet

Your hands and feet, from your fingers to your toes, need more attention than you might think. Keeping them clean and well-groomed is an important part of caring for your body.

Wash Up!

Think of all the different ways you use your hands and fingers throughout the day, from pulling your hair back in a ponytail to writing the answers to a pop quiz. With all this use, your hands can get dirty and pick up microscopic bacteria, so it's important to wash them regularly with soap and water to keep germs from spreading from your hands to your mouth, nose, or eyes.

That means you should wash your hands every time you use the bathroom, before you eat, before you cook anything, before you put your contacts in, when you handle garbage (your cat is cute, but that kitty litter is full of germs!), when you use public transportation, after you blow your nose . . . I could go on and on, but you get the idea. You should also be sure to wash your hands a lot when you're sick or when you're around someone who's sick. To really get your hands clean, lather up for about twenty seconds, rinse well, and dry.

Confessions of a Nail Biter

When I was younger, I was a nail biter. I would bite my fingernails down to the skin—it hurt, but I just couldn't stop! Sometimes, when I was watching a movie or doing homework, I would realize that I had been biting my nails without even thinking about it! My mom tried everything to help me. We painted a horrible tasting polish on my nails (it worked for a while), and I started wearing a ring that I would twist around every time I was tempted to bite. It was a good distraction, and eventually I was able to break the habit. But it took almost a year. I really had to work hard, and if you're a nail biter, you'll probably have to work on it, too.

Do You Know . . . Your Nails Are as Complex as the Rest of You?

✳ Your nails don't grow at the same speed! Your pinkie nail grows slower than the other nails.

✳ Your nails are made of a tough protein called keratin.

✳ Eating a balanced diet and drinking water will actually help your nails grow stronger and faster.

✳ Your nails grow faster in the summer than in any other season.

Biting doesn't just make your nails look bad, it's also bad for your health. Your hands carry a lot of germs, so those germs go into your body every time you put your hands in your mouth.

If you are a nail biter or have a habit like sucking your thumb or your fingers, you *can* stop. It will take time, but with help from your parents and a lot of effort on your part, you'll be able to break the habit, and it will feel great when you do!

How to Deal with a Hangnail, Callus, or Wart

You're bound to encounter one of these issues at some point, but happily, none of them is a big problem.

✳ **Hangnails:** A hangnail is when dead skin pulls away from the nail and is left "hanging" there. Never pull or pick at a hangnail, since this can tear the healthy skin and can cause an infection. Instead, soak the finger in warm water to soften the skin. Using clean nail clippers, cut the hangnail off and let the area heal.

✳ **Calluses:** When there is friction against the skin for a long period of time, your body grows extra layers of skin, creating a thick, tough spot—or callus—for protection. Calluses usually look whitish or grayish and can feel dry and scratchy. You usually get them from a repetitive activity, like gripping the handle of a tennis racket or even holding a video game controller. And you probably have them on the bottoms of your feet and on your writing finger, too. Since calluses are your body's way of protecting itself, don't worry about getting rid of them, especially if they make it easier to do something you love—like grip the uneven bars for a great gymnastics routine!

✳ **Warts:** Warts are small skin-colored bumps that usually show up on hands and feet. They are caused by a virus and you can get them from accidentally touching someone else's wart or an object someone with warts has touched. That's why gyms and locker rooms, where people walk barefoot, are common places to catch warts. You might have heard fairy tales that feature mean witches who had warts on their noses, but in real life, warts aren't dangerous or scary, and they usually go away on their own. You can treat warts with medicine from the drugstore or see your doctor about having them removed.

Foot Care 101

Trim Those Toenails: Since toenails grow much slower than fingernails, you don't need to trim them as often. When you do, cut them straight across, just like your fingernails, smoothing down any jagged edges with a file. And remember, keep those feet and toenails clean!

Ingrown Nails: When the edge of your finger or toenail grows into the skin, this causes tenderness and sometimes infection. It's more common to get ingrown toenails because shoes, especially tight-fitting or pointy-toed styles, can put pressure on the nail. Preventing ingrown nails is one of the main reasons you should trim them straight across—rounding the edges can cause nails to grow into the skin. Lightly ingrown nails should be trimmed closely. Since it's hard to do this on your own nails and get the right angle with the clippers, you might want someone to help you. An infected ingrown nail should be treated by a doctor.

Shoes That Fit: Growth spurts can affect your feet, too! One girl I know said she grew three shoe sizes in one year! If your shoes are feeling tight or your arches are hurting, you might need to go shopping. You don't want cramped feet to cramp your style!

Blisters: Have you ever worn shoes that were too small and had a sore red spot on your heel or pinkie toe at the end of the day? These spots are blisters, and they are caused by something rubbing or putting pressure on your skin. Blisters usually heal on their own, so don't pop them. Just cover the spot with an adhesive bandage until it heals.

Fresh and Foot-tastic!

Smelly gym shoes? Your feet sweat just like your armpits and when they sweat in your shoes, it can really stink!

✱ **Keep It Fresh:** Be sure you always wear clean socks. Smelly shoes come from bacteria that can't get out into the air, so wear cotton socks to let your feet breathe. Wearing shoes without socks makes them smell more quickly, since there's nothing between your feet and the shoes to keep your feet from sweating directly on them.

✱ **Get Rid of the Smell:** Sprinkle a little baby powder inside your shoes to dry things up and make them smell cleaner. Another trick is to put your shoes outside overnight (or for a few days) when it's really cold. The cold will freeze and kill the bacteria and should take some of the smell away.

✱ **Athlete's Foot:** If your feet are itchy and irritated, or if the skin is flaking, you might have athlete's foot—a fungus that grows in damp, moist environments (like shoes and feet!). Most girls get athlete's foot from walking barefoot in gyms, shower areas, and locker rooms. Wearing flip-flops in public showers can help prevent it, and it can easily be cured with the right medicine from a pharmacist or doctor.

CHAPTER THREE
Bust-ed!
Buds, Breasts, and Bras

When I talk to girls about puberty, breasts are one of the main topics that come up. And it makes sense! Breasts are a major part of your body development, and they usually start growing a year or so before you start your period, which makes them one of the first changes you have to deal with.

But you won't have to adjust to having breasts overnight. It often takes about five years, with many of the big changes happening during the first two years, for your breasts to really start taking shape. It's in these first few years that you will notice your breast buds starting to grow and you will start to wear a bra.

Breast Buds

When you're a little girl, your chest is mostly flat. That will change when you start growing "breast buds." I always thought this was a funny phrase, and I pictured my breasts budding into flowers when my mom told me about it. But don't worry. You aren't going to grow roses or daffodils on your chest.

Many girls start growing breast buds between the ages of seven and twelve, although you don't need to worry if you start earlier or later. Just like the other changes that come with puberty, your breasts will grow at the time that is right for your body.

You'll know your breast buds are developing when you feel something behind your nipples starting to push your nipples out a little bit, although your nipples themselves will stay mostly flat.

The Five Stages of Breast Development

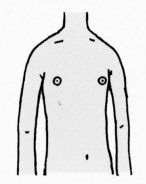

Stage 1: Childhood—You haven't started puberty, so your chest is totally flat.

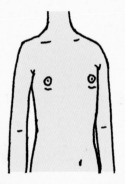

Stage 2: Breast Buds—Small lumps of tissue begin to form behind your nipples.

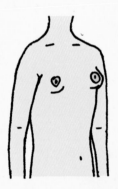

Stage 3: Growing—For the next six months to a year, your breast buds grow softer and slightly larger. Your nipples and areolae (the colored circle on your breast surrounding the nipple) get darker and larger, too.

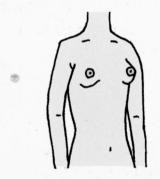

Stage 4: Still Growing!—For the next few years, your breasts will continue growing. You will probably need to get different bras during this time as your breasts get bigger.

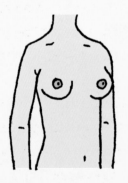

Stage 5: Fully Grown Breasts—The final stage is when you are fully developed. This is usually about three to five years after you first develop breast buds, but it can take longer. It's different for every girl.

At the beginning, breast buds usually feel like small, hard lumps. One girl I talked to said her breast buds felt like tiny golf balls behind her nipples. Another said hers felt more like quarters. No matter how yours feel, after about six months or a year, your breast buds will swell and start growing softer and wider. When they extend past your nipples and areolae, your breast buds are becoming breasts!

What Is an Areola?

The circle of skin around the nipple is called the areola (pronounced like air-ee-oh-la). Your areolae will get darker and larger as your breasts grow, but their size and color will be different from girl to girl. During puberty, some girls start to have hair grow on their areolae.

When you start developing breast buds, you'll probably notice your nipples more than before. Eventually, your nipples will stick out more than when you were young. Some girls have inverted nipples, which means their nipples retract a little bit into their breasts instead of pointing outward.

During puberty, some girls' nipples and areolae form a slight second bump on their growing breasts. This is totally normal, and the bumps will even out as you grow—they are nothing to stress about.

Beyond the Buds—Still Growing and Growing!

For the next few years, your breasts will continue growing and becoming softer. Your nipples and areolae will also get larger and darker during this stage. You may not notice big changes day-to-day, because this all happens slowly, just like everything else on your body.

Girl Talk:
How to Handle Being an Early Bird

Dear Sarah,
No one else at school has breasts yet, but mine are huge.
Boys tease me, and I feel like everyone notices them.
What can I do? Please help!
    Mariana

Dear Mariana,
I was just like you. I developed early, and I felt like everyone noticed. But don't worry—this stage won't last forever, and chances are, even though you think everyone is focused on you, they are probably more worried about what people are thinking of them!

    I understand that you feel self-conscious. When those boys tease you, just ignore them and, if you can, find a friend who will leave the situation with you. It might sound crazy, but the people who pick on you are the people who don't have any confidence in themselves. Don't listen to them!

xxx Sarah

Girl Talk:
How to Handle Being a Late Bloomer

Dear Sarah,
I'm in eighth grade, and all of my friends have bras, but I don't have one yet. My mom says I don't need one, but my sister wore one by the time she was my age. Will my boobs ever grow? When will I finally be able to wear a bra?
Taylor

Dear Taylor,
It sounds like you feel a little left behind. But don't worry! You WILL develop and need a bra when the time is right for your body. I wish I could tell you exactly when that will be, but every girl is different, and your breasts will grow when your body is ready for them.

If you feel ready for a training bra, you should definitely talk to your mom about it. Together, the two of you can discuss when you need to start wearing one and maybe even look for a bra that is right for you in these beginning stages. In the meantime, you might want to try wearing a camisole or thin tank top underneath your shirts for support.

But don't worry about keeping up with your friends or sister. Everyone is different. Try to appreciate your body for all of the great things it does for you and remember that your breasts will come, probably sooner than you think!

xxx Sarah

Sizing Things Up

Have you ever looked at a garden and noticed that every flower, even from the same plant, is a different size? It's the same way with women and breasts—even with women who are related. Your mom or sister might have large breasts, and yours might be small. Or you might end up with larger breasts than your mom. You might start out with the same size breasts as your best friend, but hers might grow bigger than yours. Or vice versa! Some girls get caught up with the idea that they want a certain size of breasts. But just like you can't control your height or shoe size, you can't change the size of your natural breasts. Part of growing up is becoming comfortable and confident about who you are and appreciating how amazing your body is. Don't get caught up in the idea that one size of breasts (or one size of anything!) is *perfect* or *better*. Your body is just right for you.

MYTH BUSTER: Sleeping on Your Stomach Won't Change Your Breast Size

Sleeping on your stomach won't flatten your breasts or affect your breast size at all. And sleeping on one side or the other won't make them lopsided. (I've heard that rumor, too!) Just go with whatever position is most comfortable, because you definitely need a good night's sleep to keep your body growing. *ZZZzzz . . .*

Shape Up!

We tend to think of breasts in pairs, like matching socks, but breasts are individual, which means they come in all different shapes and sizes. Every single girl has a slightly different shape, so there's no such thing as "normal."

If one of your breasts seems a little larger or smaller than the other, don't worry. As your body is growing, you need to give it time to even things out, and even when your breasts are fully developed, chances are they won't be exactly the same.

If you are really worried about your breast size (or anything else), you can always talk to an adult you trust or a doctor. Remember, they are here to help you. Chances are, everyone else is wondering the exact same thing or has had the same question at some point.

Sensitive Breasts?

Sometimes when your breasts are growing, they might feel a little tender or sore. They also might feel itchy or sensitive, and this can happen because your skin is stretching. These kinds of discomforts are all part of the growing process and really nothing to worry about. Basically, as your breasts swell, the hormones in your system and the nerves in your breasts can make them feel a little achy. You can put lotion on itchy skin, and any tenderness shouldn't last too long. If you are worried about soreness or pain, it's a good idea to talk to your mom and your doctor. Your doctor will be able to help you figure out what's causing the pain and what to do about it.

Girl Talk:
What Are These Lines on My Breasts?

Dear Sarah,
Pinkish purple lines started forming on my breasts in the last few months. Are these veins? What should I do to make them go away?
    Emma

Dear Emma,
The lines you've noticed are stretch marks and nothing you should worry about. You are basically growing so fast your skin can't keep up. This happens to a lot of girls, and many girls get stretch marks on their hips, thighs, and bottoms, too. These areas of your body are rounding out during puberty, which is why your skin stretches there. While you can't do anything to make stretch marks go away, they will fade as you keep grow- ing. You might see lotions and creams at the store that promise to remove stretch marks, but don't buy that claim. Only Mother Nature and time will help your skin tone even out.

XXX Sarah

Bra Basics

Most girls start wearing a bra around the time they enter into stage three, the growing stage, of breast development. In addition to giving your growing breasts some support, the soft fabric of a bra can help protect your tender skin and nipples as your breasts grow. A bra can also give you some coverage as your nipples start to become noticeable through your shirts.

Most bras have adjustable straps so you can lengthen or shorten them for your shoulder and body height. Move them around to find the most comfortable length.

Most bras also have hook closures in the back to keep the elastic band in place (although some hook in the front between your breasts). Adjustable hooks are good, because you can decide which one to use for the right fit as you grow. Don't worry if it takes you a while to get used to fastening the hooks—you'll get the hang of it!

The cups are where your breasts go when you are wearing the bra. You want the cups snug but not tight. If your breasts fill the cups to overflowing, you should probably get a size larger. If there's a lot of space between your skin and the cups, you should probably go down a size.

The elastic band goes around your rib cage (below your breasts) and stretches so it's comfortable to wear.

Shopping for Your First Bra

When I asked Norah Alberto, the senior style director at Maidenform (a major bra company), for tips on shopping for a first bra, she suggested that you make it a "special and memorable experience." It's an important day when you get your first bra! And why not enjoy it a little? My mom and I went out for a girls-only lunch after we bought my first bra. I didn't want to make a big deal out if it, but the lunch was super fun and something I will never forget. You can also do something yourself to remember the day, such as write in your diary or treat yourself to a bubble bath. Whatever feels fun for you!

Do You Know . . .
When Bras Were Invented?

Girls have been wearing bras for centuries! Historians say that the first bra dates way back to the Minoan civilization in 2500 BC. But it wasn't until the 1930s that adjustable bands were invented.

It's All About the Fit:

Finding Your Bra Size

Even though there are a lot of websites that sell bras for teens, it's best to buy your first bra in person, so you can try on a few for fit and feel. Most stores have a good selection of bras made especially for teens and girls who are just starting to develop. Norah Alberto suggests experimenting with some of the cute prints and patterns and fun colors that are out there. (I love cotton bras because they let your skin breathe and they wash and wear well.)

A Professional Fitting

Unlike pants or T-shirts, which usually come in small, medium, and large, bra sizes are designated by a combination of the distance around your rib cage and your bust size (the circumference of your chest measured around the widest part of your breasts). The combo sizing makes things a bit complicated, which is why it can be helpful to get a professional bra fitting. Any department store should have a bra-fitting specialist—an expert in finding the right size for you.

But, as if shopping for a bra isn't embarrassing enough (even if you want one!), the fitting process can be a little awkward if you don't know what to expect. So here's what will happen:

Usually, the bra-fitting specialist will go with you to the dressing room, so you have a little privacy. You can keep your shirt on (although if you're wearing a bulky sweater, you might want to have a T-shirt or cami underneath for the measuring). The fitting specialist will wrap a measuring tape around your rib cage and then around your breasts to get the two different measurements—for the band size and the cup size. You need both to get a bra that fits well.

Chances are, a parent or someone you're close to will go with you to get a bra fitted. There's no need to be embarrassed about the fitting process. If your mom or stepmom is with you, she's been through it, too. And the woman working at the department store has done tons of fittings! She just wants to help you find the most comfortable bra for your body.

Fitting Yourself

Even though a professional fitting is helpful, you can also measure yourself. All you need is a measuring tape with inches on it. (Bra sizes differ depending on where you live! This information applies to American sizes, though U.K. sizes are very similar—they're even in inches. If you're wondering exactly what size bra you'd wear in the United Kingdom, or in Japan, for example, just reference one of the many international bra size converters online!)

All bra sizes are made up of an even number for the band size (like 30, 32, 34, 36, and so on) and a letter for the cup size (A, B, C, D, and then into double letters for larger breasts).

Bra Sizing 101

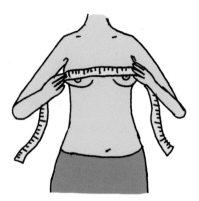

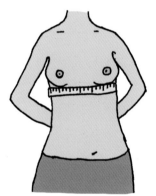

1) **Measure Your Bust Line:** Lift your arms away from your body and wrap a measuring tape with inch markings around the point where your breasts are largest. You should be able to get a finger between the measuring tape and your skin without a problem. Look at the number where the measuring tape meets. This is your bust measure.

2) **Measure Your Band Size:** Lift your arms away from your body and wrap the measuring tape around your torso just below your breasts. Look at the number where the measuring tape meets. If it's an odd number, round up to the next even number. For instance, if you measure 33 inches around, you will wear a size 34. If it's an even number, this is your band size (but you should try the size up, too, to see which is more comfortable).

3) **Math Time:** Put your math skills to work and subtract your band size from your bust measure.

Bust line measurement – band size measurement = cup size

(the number of inches you have left over will determine your cup size)

Cup Sizes

AA Cup = less than ½ inch of difference between the band and bust size measurements

A Cup = ½ to 1 inch of difference

B Cup = 2 inches of difference

C Cup = 3 inches of difference

D Cup = 4 inches of difference

If your band size is 30 inches and your bust is 2 inches larger than that, you should start by trying on bras tagged size 30B. Since every bra is a little different, you might need to try on different styles and brands to find the right one. It's also good to remember that as your breasts grow, your bra size will change. You'll want to get refitted or measure yourself again each time you shop for a new bra.

The right bra won't hurt your shoulders or pull too tight around your chest or rib cage. It shouldn't gap underneath your arms or in the cups when you are standing straight. A bra that's too small will feel tight and painful. You want one that lets you breathe but still helps hold your breasts in place.

A bra is a personal thing, and you might be surprised that you like a different style of bra than your sister or friend, but it makes sense: Every body is different.

The Best Bra for Every Activity

In addition to a good fit, you want to make sure you're wearing the right bra for the right activity so that you can be comfortable and your breasts are held in place. You wouldn't wear your soccer cleats to ballet class, and you definitely wouldn't wear your ski boots to school. Bras are the same way! Sometimes, when you don't have the right support, your breasts can become tender and sore, and that's definitely no fun.

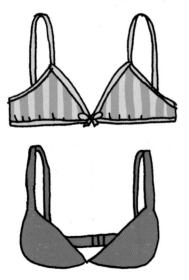

✳ **Training Bra:** These bras are for girls who are just starting to develop, though you aren't actually training for anything! They are specifically made out of comfortable fabrics and in smaller cup sizes, all good for getting you used to wearing a bra. Training bras are sometimes called "bralettes."

✳ **T-Shirt Bra:** T-shirt bras don't have seams in the cups or an elastic band, so you won't be able to see any lines under your T-shirt. These are great everyday bras, often made out of breathable cotton.

✷   **Sports Bra:** This bra is for—you got it— sports! It's also for anytime you want a little extra support. It is made to hold your breasts firmly in place during physical activity, from basketball to dance class to running around with your friends. Sports bras are usually made from very stretchy material like spandex, and you usually just pull them over your head (there aren't any clasps).

A lot of girls think sports bras are the most comfortable, and if you feel this way, you can definitely wear them all the time. There's no need to save them just for sports!

✷   **Underwire Bra:** An underwire bra has actual U-shaped wires under each of the cups to give added support. For proper fit when wearing an underwire bra, make sure that the wires lie flat against your rib cage.

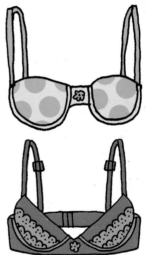

✷   **Lined or Padded Bra:** You can get a bra with a thick lining or light padding for extra coverage. Some women, when they get older, wear padded bras to get more shape.

✷   **T-Back or Racer-Back Bra:** This bra has straps that run down the middle of your back to form a T, instead of coming down behind each of your shoulders, much like a racing swimsuit. If you ever get shoulder pain from wearing a bra, this style can help balance the weight from your breasts across your back. This is also a good bra to wear with a racer-back tank top or if your bra straps slip off your shoulders.

✳ **Bandeau Bra / Strapless Bra:** A bandeau bra wraps around your breasts like a tube. Some pull over your head and others fasten with hooks in the back. Since they're strapless, they don't offer a ton of support, but they are good for layering clothes or if you have a shirt with low armholes and want to make sure something is covering the sides of your body. You can also get strapless bras with underwire.

✳ **Built-in Bra:** Many shirts and tops (swimsuits, too) have bras built into them. These are sometimes called "shelf" bras because they hold up your breasts like they are on a shelf. (I always giggle at that description—when would it ever be comfortable to have a shelf under your breasts?!) If you want extra support and coverage, you can also wear another bra when you are wearing a shirt that has a built-in bra.

Bra Care

"Always let a bra rest between wearings," suggests Norah Alberto. And when it comes to washing your bras, it's a good idea to wash them every few wears. They get sweaty just like the rest of your clothes!

If you have any bras that are made of delicate fabric, like lace or even cotton with stretch, you might want to wash them separately from the rest of your clothes to help them last longer. It's also a good idea to hang your bras to dry, since the dryer can wear out the elastic in stretch fabrics, bend the underwire in underwire bras, and snag delicate fabrics; sometimes the heat can even cause bras to shrink!

Where to Wear Which Bra?

Not sure which bra to wear, when? Here are some good suggestions, whatever you might be doing.

If you are . . .		You might want to wear . . .
going to ballet rehearsal	→	a sports bra or racer-back bra
hanging out with friends on Saturday	→	a T-shirt bra (great for every day!)
wearing a cute dress	→	a lined bra, or if you need support, an underwire
playing softball at the park	→	a sports bra, since you'll be running the bases
going to school	→	whichever bra is most comfortable for a full day
riding your bike	→	a sports bra or a top with a built-in bra
going shopping with your mom	→	a T-shirt bra (the best for trying on all kinds of clothes)
wearing a tank top with low-cut armholes	→	a bandeau bra
going to bed	→	you don't need to sleep in a bra but some girls like to wear shirts with built-in bras to bed

How Many Bras Is Enough?

To know how many bras you need, think about what kinds of activities you do. If you play a lot of sports, then you might want a few sports bras, as well as some other bras that you can wear with regular clothes. It's kind of a personal thing. Norah Alberto recommends having "a couple of T-shirt bras, a T-back bra, a bralette, and a sports bra to round out your bra wardrobe."

White or skin-colored bras are best for wearing under white shirts, and a dark or black bra is good under dark shirts and sweaters. One time, a friend took a picture of me while I was wearing a white bra under a black T-shirt. You couldn't tell in real life, but the flash from the camera caught the white fabric, and in the photo, you could see my bright white bra through my shirt!

 GET CONFIDENT: Your First Bra

In fifth grade, I had just started wearing a bra and was fidgeting with the straps in class one day. A boy noticed and said loudly, "I just saw your bra strap! You wear a bra!"

I was mortified. I hadn't even told my friends that I was wearing a bra yet! A few kids laughed, but I just said, "Whatever," and went back to working on my math problem. Really, I was so embarrassed, I felt like crying.

At lunch, my friend Anna came up and whispered in my ear, "Don't worry. I started wearing a bra, too." She smiled, and suddenly I realized that I wasn't alone. Just because we hadn't talked about getting bras didn't mean that we weren't both going through the same thing. Remember, all girls go through puberty, and even when things feel scary or uncomfortable, you are never alone.

A Note from Sarah:
Your Body Is Yours

While we're talking about your body and developing, it's also important to remember that your body is yours, and no one should ever touch you without 100 percent permission. You are in charge of your body. NO ONE, no matter how well you know them, has the right to do anything to your body. You always have the right to feel comfortable and safe.

If anyone—either an adult or another kid—tries to touch you in a way that makes you feel uncomfortable AT ALL, you should immediately tell an adult you trust. Don't wait, and don't feel embarrassed. It's never your fault if someone tries to take advantage of you—turn to the people who love you and want to help you.

Remember to trust your feelings. If you have a bad feeling about something or someone, it's better to talk about it than ignore it. A trusted adult will help keep you safe. Everyone has the right to protect her own body. Be sure you demand respect for yours and respect other people as well.

xxx Sarah

CHAPTER FOUR

Let's Talk, Period

What You Need to Know About Menstruation

For most girls, getting their period is the biggest moment in the entire puberty process. Sure, your breasts will grow, and you'll probably have a growth spurt. You start wearing deodorant, and you might start shaving your legs. But getting your period—that's a big deal, even compared to all of that other important stuff!

Getting your period is a rite of passage. It's a physical sign that you are becoming a woman, because it's an important part of being able to have a baby one day. That's a long ways off, but your body goes through this process now. That's why your mom or health teacher might say that once you start your period, you're a woman.

But what are the signs leading up to your first period, and what happens when you actually get it? How will you know it's started, and how long will it last? How much blood will there be? Will it hurt?

Don't worry! We are going to walk step by step through what it means to have your period so that you are prepared and confident when yours starts.

Before Your Period Starts

Pubic Hair

Before you actually start your period, your body does a number of things to prepare itself, kind of like practicing for a piano recital or shooting hoops before a basketball game. These are important steps for your maturing body and usually happen before you get your first period. One of these steps is growing pubic hair.

Your pubic area is a few inches (or 5 to 9 centimeters) below your belly button, between your hips where your legs meet.

Over the next few years, your pubic hair will grow in the shape of an upside-down triangle. You will grow hair between your legs on your vulva, the outside of your vagina. Some girls grow pubic hair on the inner, top parts of their thighs, and for some, it grows up toward the belly button.

Your pubic hair will likely start to appear about the time you begin growing armpit hair. It might be only a few fine and light-colored hairs at first. The thickness, texture, and color of pubic hair is different for each girl. It may or may not be the same color as the hair on your head. As you get older and farther into puberty, your pubic hair will get thicker, and it usually gets curly and coarse.

Discharge

After you start growing pubic hair, you might notice a milky white or clear, sticky substance in your underpants. This is called vaginal discharge, and it is released by your body because of the estrogen in your system. Estrogen is a hormone that is important for your period and eventually will help you to have children.

Girls usually see discharge six months to a year before they start their periods, but again, every girl is different. Discharge is a sign you might get your period soon, but it's not like an alarm clock that will tell you exactly when it's going to happen.

Although healthy vaginal discharge is not odorless, sometimes discharge develops a stronger odor than normal or looks thick like cottage cheese. If you notice these symptoms, or if your vagina is itchy and red, you might have an infection. Fishy or rotten-smelling discharge is like a warning sign that you need to see a doctor.

Your vagina is a place where bacteria can grow easily, because it's between your legs, doesn't get much fresh air, and is moist. Just like you clean the rest of your body, you need to wash and care for it. Beware of scented soaps, bubble baths, and perfumed lotions, which can irritate the sensitive skin of your vagina. Swimsuits, leotards, and other tight, stretchy clothing also trap bacteria, so it's a good idea to take them off right after you're done with activities.

To keep your vagina clean, wash every time you take a bath or shower. Then dry between your legs completely and wear breathable, 100 percent cotton underpants. Avoid brands that have even a tiny bit of Lycra or spandex in them, since it's hard for air to get through those fabrics. Be sure to wear a clean pair of underwear every day.

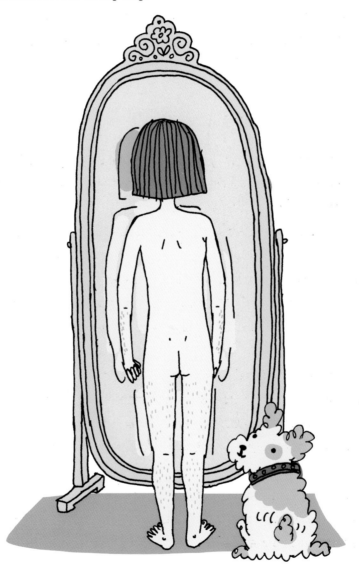

Girl Talk:
Are Certain Smells Normal?

Dear Sarah,
I have this smell coming from my undies. I have discharge,
but I haven't started my period yet. What is the smell
coming from?
    Mia

Dear Mia,
Most girls notice a slight smell coming from their vagina
after they start puberty. Our bodies just have smells;
it's part of being human. It's important to keep your
vagina clean, but you will probably always have a light
odor like what you smell now.

    You may hear about products that claim to get rid of
vaginal odor. But these aren't healthy, because the per-
fumes and other ingredients in them can cause irritation.
If you notice that the smell gets fishy or rotten, talk to
your mom. All women get infections from time to time, and
they are usually easy to clear up, but you do need to see
a doctor to get the right diagnosis and medicine.

    One other thing: Nobody notices the smell but you.
Promise! We are all in tune with our own bodies, and
smells are a way they communicate with us.

XXX Sarah

Getting Your Period

No one can predict exactly when you are going to get your first period, but it generally happens about two years after your breasts start growing and six months to a year after you start noticing vaginal discharge. It would be great if one day you woke up and your body said, "Today you will start your period." Then you would know! But it doesn't happen like that. So the best thing you can do is learn what to expect, watch for some of the signs that your body is maturing, and be prepared for when it happens.

Registered nurse Elaine Plummer works for the company that makes Tampax tampons and Always pads, and knows a lot about periods. She says "the average age for girls in the United States to begin their menstrual period is age twelve, but it's not unusual to begin as early as age eight or as late as fifteen." She says it's important to remember that every girl develops at her own pace, so even though these are general guidelines, you will get your period in your own time. If you haven't started your period by the time you turn sixteen, she says it's a good idea to visit your doctor or health care provider to make sure your body is on the right track.

What Will Actually Happen During My Period?

During your period, you bleed from your vagina. The blood comes from your uterus, which is a reproductive organ that will one day help you have a baby.

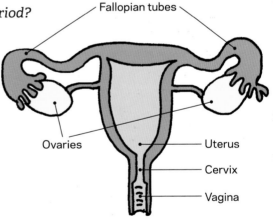

The idea of bleeding might seem scary, but it's a normal part of being a woman and not something you need to be grossed out by. And it's not like when you cut your finger. When you get your period, your body controls the whole process. It knows exactly how much and how long to bleed.

During your entire period, which will last between two and seven days, your body will lose about one to six tablespoons (15 to 90 milliliters) of blood.

What Is Menstruation?

Menstruation is the proper term for "having your period," and chances are, it's a word you will hear a lot during puberty. It comes from the Latin word for "month," which itself comes from the Greek word for "moon." This is because you usually get your period about once a month (twenty-eight days is the standard time between periods), and in some cultures, people use the roughly twenty-eight-day cycles of the moon as the basis for their calendars.

Words You've Probably Heard: **Cycle** and **Flow**

To keep your period calendar private, mark the start and stop of your period in a secret code or even a symbol like a star.

Cycle:

Your menstrual cycle is measured from the **start** of one period to the **start** of the next. The average cycle is about twenty-eight days, but it can vary from twenty-one to forty-five days in teens. Nurse Plummer says not to worry if your cycle doesn't fall into a pattern right away. "It's not unusual to have an irregular cycle for the first two years or so after you begin menstruating. Mark on a calendar when your period begins and keep track of how long it lasts. After a while, you will likely notice a pattern developing. This should make it easier to predict when your next period will begin. Once you have established a regular cycle, if your period stops happening regularly or stops completely, you should check with your doctor."

Flow:

The word *flow* is used to describe the rate of bleeding during your period. For example, if you are bleeding a lot, your flow is heavy. If you are bleeding less, your flow is light. Your flow will likely be lighter at the very beginning and end of your period, and heavier during the middle.

Girls Who've Been There:
First Period Stories

"*Throughout seventh and eighth grade, I lied to my friends that I had my period. At sleepovers, when everyone was complaining about how terrible periods, cramps, pads, and tampons were, I would say things like 'Oh, I know. Cramps are the worst!' I didn't want them to know I was the odd one out. When I actually did get my period, I felt overwhelmed. I was at my house, and my mom wasn't home! But my older sister hooked me up with everything I needed. I remember learning what a period was in third grade and then I didn't get it for another five years. I wish I had known that there was such a wide range of ages when you can get your period. Maybe then I wouldn't have felt like my timing was so off, because in reality, it wasn't.*" —Shelby

"*I got my first period in the beginning of seventh grade, but I didn't get it again for about five months! I remember my mom asking if I had actually gotten my period the first time. I did, in fact, get my period when I thought I did, but it was irregular for the first two years, which is normal but can be confusing.*" —Margaret

"*I got my period when I was fourteen, on the very first day of high school. I was convinced I would need to wear a tampon or pad all the time, for fear blood would just start pouring down my leg at any moment. But it's not like that at all. It's much more controllable than I thought it would be.*" —Paige

Getting Your First Period

I remember feeling a little scared about getting my period, because it was all unknown. It's natural to feel this way. In fact, most girls do.

When your period does start, you will probably feel dampness in your underpants. You might see blood, or you might notice small dark brownish, reddish, or nearly black spots (from dried blood). Spotting is a sign that your period is coming, and you can be prepared for a heavier flow by wearing a panty liner or pad.

Not every girl's period will begin with spotting. I didn't notice anything unusual until I went to the bathroom and there was blood in my underwear and on the toilet paper when I wiped myself. I called for my mother, and she came to the bathroom. She was happy, but I started to cry! I just felt really emotional and couldn't believe I had started. I put a pad in, and I went to the bathroom every few hours just to make sure everything was okay. After a few days, I started to get a sense of my menstrual flow and wasn't so worried about checking my pad every time I could. It takes a little while to get a feeling for your period and your body, but you'll figure it out.

IF YOU START AT SCHOOL

A lot of girls are worried about starting their periods at school. One girl told me she was scared that everyone would be able to tell, and another was worried that she would bleed through her pants. The truth is you probably won't have so much blood at first that it will seep through your clothing, and you will probably feel dampness or wetness before it gets to that point. If you feel dampness in your underwear at school, stop at the bathroom between classes or ask your teacher for permission to use the bathroom. You don't need to tell anyone why you need to go unless you want to.

It's a good idea to keep a period emergency kit in your backpack or locker. But if you start and don't have a pad handy, you can use toilet paper in the meantime. Fold the toilet paper and place it in your underpants, or wrap it around the bottom part of your underpants four or five times. This will soak up the blood until you can get a real pad.

If you start your period and don't notice until you've bled through your underwear or clothing, tie a sweatshirt or sweater around your waist. Then go to the school nurse or your teacher. They've dealt with this before and will be able to call your parents or a family friend who can bring a change of clothes. You'll be good as new when you get a fresh pair of underwear!

Feminine Hygiene Products

There are a number of feminine hygiene products you can wear during your period to protect your underpants and clothes. Pads, panty liners, and tampons help absorb the blood so it doesn't get messy.

Pads

Pads, also called sanitary napkins or maxi pads, are absorbent pieces of cloth-like material that fit into your underpants. Most have a strip of tape on the bottom that sticks right to the fabric to hold the pad in place.

Pads come in various widths and lengths so you can get the right size for your body. They also come in different absorbencies. The flow of blood at the very beginning and end of your period won't be as heavy as toward the middle, which means you will probably want a different absorbency, depending on where you are in your cycle.

* **Light Flow:** Use a panty liner. This is a thinner pad for days when your period is light but you still need some protection.

* **Regular Flow:** Use a pad. It's a good idea to change your pad every two to four hours. Any longer, and it might leak or start to smell.

* **Heavy Flow or Active Days:** Use a long pad with "wings," which wrap around your underpants and stick on the outside. The wings give a little extra support and security to keep the pad in place if you are playing sports or during the night when you are sleeping.

Don't throw your panty liners or pads away in the toilet. They will clog the plumbing. Instead, wrap them in toilet paper or tissue and put them in the garbage can. Most women's bathrooms have small garbage cans right in the bathroom stalls!

⭐ **GET CONFIDENT**: Practicing with Pads ⭐

One pediatrician I know suggests that girls practice with pads before they start their first period. Talk to your mom about getting a box of pads. Then, at home, take some time in the bathroom to practice inserting the pad comfortably into your underpants. You might want to walk around with it in for a few hours, so you can get a sense of how it will feel. This way, when you start your period, you will be prepared and confident.

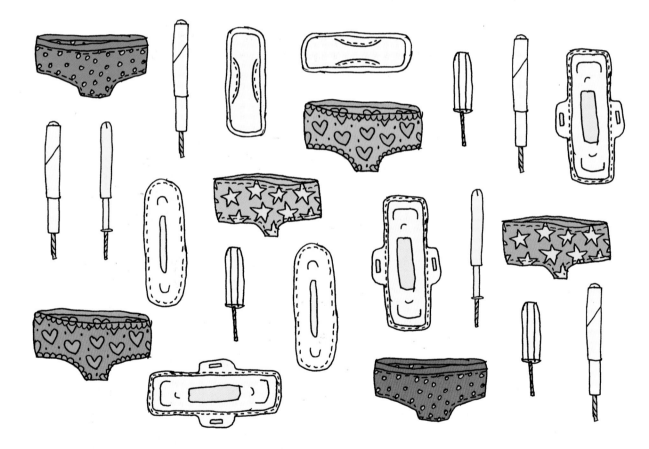

☆ GET CONFIDENT: Make a Period Preparedness Kit ☆

Since you can't be sure when your first period will come—or when it will start when you aren't yet regular—it's a good idea to keep an emergency supply or period preparedness kit in your book bag, backpack, or locker. Just knowing that you have the supplies you need can take away some of the stress about starting your period, especially at school.

If you think you've started your period and don't want everyone to know why you are going to the bathroom, you can tuck a pad into your pocket or shirtsleeve before you walk from your desk to the bathroom.

➡ You can keep everything discreet by putting your period preparedness kit in a cute pencil case, a small makeup bag, or even a brown paper bag.

Period Gear Checklist

○ 2 or 3 pads

○ 2 or 3 panty liners

○ A clean change of underwear

○ 2 or 3 tampons (if you want them)

○ A bag to hold everything

Tampons

Tampons are another form of absorbent feminine hygiene product. They are inserted into your vagina and absorb the blood from inside your body. Tampons are shaped like thin, solid tubes and are made of cotton and other absorbent material. They have a thin string on the end that hangs outside your body when the tampon is in your vagina, so that you can pull it out when you need to.

Tampons come in various sizes and absorbencies, like slender, regular, and super. These sizes tell you how big the tampon is and also how absorbent it is. Some companies offer a version created especially for light flow days; these are also good for girls who are just learning to use tampons, because they are small and easy to insert. Tampons come with different types of applicators. The applicator is the piece of cardboard or plastic that covers the actual tampon and helps it slide into your vagina. Some tampons don't have applicators, and you use your finger to push them into place. These require a little more practice, so you might want to use a kind that comes with an applicator until you get the hang of the process.

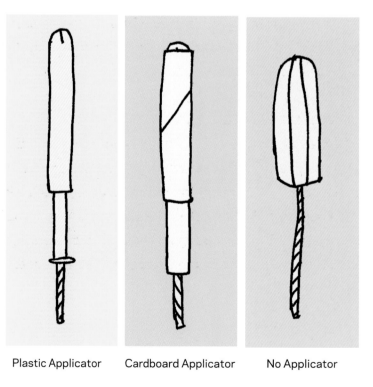

Plastic Applicator   Cardboard Applicator   No Applicator

 To help cut down on waste and keep the planet healthy, use tampons with cardboard or biodegradable applicators—some companies even make applicators from recycled materials!

WHEN TO START USING TAMPONS

There's no specific age when a girl can start using tampons. It is a personal decision, and you don't have to make it right when you start your period. You can get used to pads first, and then, when you feel ready, make the change to using tampons. Many women use tampons and pads at the same time, and some women choose not to use tampons at all.

When Nurse Plummer's daughter started to menstruate, her advice was, "Your period is manageable and should not interrupt your life in any way. Tampons help with that." It's an important lesson to remember because, yes, your period is new and it's a big deal, but it shouldn't stop your life. You can still do the same things you did before it started.

Like anything, practice makes things easier, and you will need to practice inserting a tampon before you get the hang of it. To help this process go more smoothly for you, Nurse Plummer shared some of her first-time tampon tips, and I've added a few tips of my own.

HOW DO YOU KNOW IF IT'S IN CORRECTLY?

When the tampon is in, a few inches (or 5 to 9 centimeters) of the string should be visible and hanging between your thighs. When you stand up, you shouldn't be able to feel the tampon. If it hurts, it probably isn't far enough into the vagina, or it might be off center. Remove it by pulling the string and start over with a fresh tampon. Keep practicing until you can't feel the tampon inside. Then wash your hands, and you are done!

Tampons 101: How to Insert a Tampon

1) Gather up your supplies: a few slender or junior-size tampons, a small mirror (a compact makeup mirror is great for this), some water-based vaginal lubricant (you can find this at the drugstore or ask your parents for help, but definitely don't use Vaseline or petroleum jelly!), and some patience. Make sure you have plenty of time for this first session. Rushing through it will make the process frustrating!

2) Wash your hands with soap and water and make sure your vaginal area is clean. You don't want to get bacteria inside your vagina, since that could lead to an infection. Then sit down on the toilet.

3) Use the hand mirror to help you see what you're doing. You might need to use your fingers to gently separate the folds of the labia.

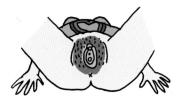

4) You'll see two openings—the first, highest hole, is the urethra (where you urinate from), the second is your vagina, where you will insert the tampon. You can still use the bathroom normally while using tampons.

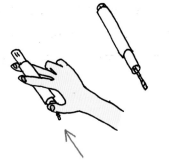

5) Unwrap the wrapper. Holding the applicator with your thumb and first two fingers, insert the round tip of the applicator slightly into your vagina.

6) Gently push the applicator into your vagina at a slight upward angle (not straight up or back). After the outer tube of the applicator is inserted all the way, push up the inner tube with your forefinger. This positions the tampon up into your vagina.

7) Pull the entire applicator out, wrap it in toilet paper, and throw it in the trash can (not the toilet).

Hint: If you are having a hard time pushing the tampon in, add a few drops of lubricant to the tip of the applicator. This can help moisten the sensitive skin of your labia so it doesn't hurt when you insert the tampon. Get a new tampon if you need to. It can take a few tries to get this process down.

REMOVING THE TAMPON

After four to six hours, it's time to remove the tampon. Take a deep breath to relax your vaginal muscles and pull down gently on the string. The tampon will slide out of your vagina. You can wrap it in toilet paper and throw it away in the garbage. Some bathrooms have strong enough plumbing systems to handle flushing a tampon, but to be safe, throw away used tampons.

I remember worrying that the string would get lost or get stuck inside my body and I wouldn't be able to get the tampon out, but the truth is you can still remove a tampon, even if you can't find the string, by using your fingers to gently pull it out.

Some of the symptoms of TSS are like the flu, but they can become serious quickly. If you are experiencing these symptoms, especially if you're using tampons at the time, tell an adult and talk to your doctor right away.

* Rising body temperature (102 degrees Fahrenheit /38.8 degrees Celsius or higher) * Vomiting * Diarrhea
* A sunburn-like rash * Muscle aches
* Dizziness * Fainting or near fainting when you stand up

Once, at a sleepover, a friend told me that sometimes a tampon can get stuck or lost inside you, but that's a total myth. There's no chance that a tampon can get lost in your body. The only other opening inside your vagina is your cervix, and—unless you're in the middle of giving birth to a baby—the opening is so small that only liquid can get through. A tampon can only enter and leave your body through your vagina.

Nurse Plummer says, "Never wear a tampon for more than eight hours, and remember to remove the last tampon you put in at the end of your period." You can sleep with a tampon, but she suggests you use the lowest absorbency you can, and that you use a pad if you sleep longer than eight hours.

Wearing a tampon can lead to a very rare but serious bacterial disease called Toxic Shock Syndrome (TSS). Tampons don't actually cause TSS; for reasons still not fully understood, your body can produce a substance that causes TSS when you use them. Your vagina is a potential breeding ground for bacteria, and inserting an absorbent tampon and leaving it for a long time seems to create favorable conditions for certain dangerous types of bacteria. To reduce the risk of TSS, it's important that you do not leave a tampon in for longer than eight hours and that you use the lowest absorbency tampons you can, even if it means changing them more frequently. It is also important to know the signs and symptoms of TSS, and to remove your tampon and call your doctor if you experience these while using a tampon—as long as TSS is recognized early and treated promptly, it is nearly always curable. Every box of tampons also comes with information on TSS, and it's a good idea to read this material.

What Else Happens During Your Period? Cramps, Moodiness, and Bloating
Many girls notice side effects like cramps, moodiness, and acne before and during their periods. That's because your body is reacting to all the hormones in

Girl Talk: What Is PMS?

Dear Sarah,
When my sister is in a bad mood, she says she is PMS'ing. What does that mean? Will I start PMS'ing when I start my period?
   Kimora

Dear Kimora,
PMS stands for *premenstrual syndrome*. When you have your period, you are menstruating. A few days before your period actually starts, when you are in "pre" menstruation, your body releases hormones that are important for your cycle. These hormones can make you feel moody. Some girls also get tender breasts, headaches, backaches, acne breakouts, and anxiety.

   It sounds like your sister is experiencing moodiness as a PMS symptom. You might also feel moody, or your body might react differently. Keeping track of your period will help you know when to expect your period, and if you find yourself feeling anxious or stressed or even a little achy before it starts, you'll know why!

xxx Sarah

your system—hormones that make your period possible. Take it easy on your body, and your brain, when it's your time of the month. Make sure that you get enough sleep, get some fresh air, get some exercise (moving your body is great when you feel achy from your period), and eat healthy foods (salty foods can add to that puffy or bloated feeling that can come along with your period). Extra sugar and caffeine also increase cramps, so it's a good idea to stay away from them, too.

How to Handle Cramps

Many teenage girls get cramps—aching or intense pain in their lower belly area or backs—just before they start their period or during the first day or two of their cycle. Cramps are caused when your uterus, an important reproductive organ, contracts and expands. Imagine it like a fist opening and closing inside you.

As a teen, I got really bad cramps, and a few times my stomach hurt so badly I had to call my mom to come get me from school. The spot below my belly button had a sharp, almost piercing pain, and I had to bend over or curl up in the fetal position while it lasted. The pain would last a few minutes, then go away for a bit, and come back every half hour for a few hours.

For some girls, cramps will be more of a dull pain or tightness that lasts for a day or so. It's also common to get headaches or a little bit of nausea. Other girls don't get cramps at all.

Taking a warm bath or using a heating pad for a little while on the places that are cramping (like your abdomen or lower back) can help ease the pain. Exercise is good for cramps, so if you feel up for it, go on a walk or shoot some hoops. There are also medicines that can help reduce intense cramps. If your cramps are really painful or make you sick, talk to your parents or doctor about getting something to help ease the pain and other symptoms. It's not fun to be in pain every time you get your period!

Sarah's Tip: Stretch It Out

Over the years, I've found that stretching is one of the best things I can do to help relieve cramps. These are two mellow stretches I do whenever I have cramps.

1) Knees-to-Chest Stretch: Lie on your back on the floor or on your bed. Hug your knees to your chest and hold them there gently for fifteen to twenty seconds. Be sure to breathe! Then release and let your legs extend straight out. Take a few breaths and do it again two or three times.

2) Child's Pose: This one is a yoga pose. (I love doing yoga when I have cramps. It's a good form of exercise and also helps relax the muscles in my entire body.)

Start with your hands and knees on the floor, your back flat like a tabletop. Spread your knees out about 6 inches (or 15 centimeters), and touch your big toes together. Slowly lower your stomach to the floor and bring your butt back past your knees (almost like you are squatting). Extend your arms out in front so you can feel the stretch in your lower back.

Hold the pose for twenty to thirty seconds and then come back up to your hands and knees. You can repeat the pose. Remember to keep breathing the entire time and listen to your body. If something hurts, don't do it.

Dealing with a Heavy Period at Night

It's frustrating to wake up and find that you've bled through your pajamas. And it's even more frustrating when you bleed on your sheets! To help prevent it, check to see if you need to move your pad forward or backward. (You will get an idea of this based on where it looks like the blood leaked through.) You can get extra-long pads for nighttime use and wear a pair of shorts or slightly tighter pajama pants at night to help keep your underwear and pad in place if you move around a lot when you sleep.

If you wake up and there's blood on your pajamas or sheets (or if you get spots in your underwear or on your clothes during the day), rinse out the blood with cold water and then use fabric soap or put them in the washing machine. Be sure to set it for a cold water wash, since hot water sets bloodstains in fabric. Get a parent to help you with the washing, but do it as soon as you notice the stains. The sooner you get the blood rinsed out, the better chance you have of it not staining permanently!

MYTH BUSTER: You Can Still Go Swimming While on Your Period

I was on the summer swim team growing up and heard from some girls in the locker room that you couldn't come to practice or swim in the meets when you had your period. Luckily, that's just a rumor. You can definitely swim when you have your period, but it's best to swim with a tampon. A pad will get wet and absorb water instead of your menstrual blood, and if you go swimming without a tampon, you risk having blood become visible when you get out of the water. Wearing a tampon will block your flow and isn't obvious in your swimming suit.

Bathing and Showering During Your Period

A few girls asked me if they could still take a bath or shower while they were having their periods, and the answer is YES! If you take a bath, there might be some blood in the water, so some girls would rather shower when it's their time of the month. You can also put a tampon in before a bath, but it's not necessary. And don't worry about blood running down your leg while you're in the shower. Any discharge or blood will be easily washed down the drain with the flowing water.

Don't worry if all this advice seems like a lot right now. Whether you've started your period yet or not, you'll figure out what works best for you and your body. Just be patient and give yourself some time. And remember that even though it might sometimes feel overwhelming, growing up is exciting, too!

CHAPTER FIVE
Be Good to Your Body
All About Healthy Habits

Part of becoming a grown-up is learning to take care of yourself. Your parents and loved ones will still be around to help, but as you get older and go through puberty, you become more responsible for your body, and that means developing habits that will help you stay healthy and strong.

Drinking lots of water and eating healthy foods will keep your body going and growing, while getting exercise and a good night's sleep will rejuvenate your body and mind. It sounds pretty easy, and it is! Understanding the science behind the vitamins and nutrients your body needs and the biology of how your body works makes it pretty interesting, too!

It Starts with Nutrition

You don't have to tell your body to absorb a certain amount of vitamin A or to get all the calcium out of the milk you drink, do you? Your body is smart enough to know how to do that on its own. All you have to do is eat healthy, nutritious foods, and let your body do the rest.

I talked to Nora Lisman, a certified nutritionist, and she said, "What we eat affects us in so many ways. Our food choices impact everything from our energy levels in gym class to our ability to focus in math. They even impact whether we totally blow up at our mom or at a friend!" (I get cranky when I'm hungry, so I can totally relate to that.)

Calcium, which is found in dairy products (like milk, yogurt, and cheese), in dark, leafy greens (like collard greens and kale), and in soy beans and white beans, is especially important for growing girls, since it helps build and strengthen bones. Having high bone density is really important later in life, and these are the years when you determine how strong your bones will be.

What Are Healthy Foods?

There's a lot of advice out in the world on what's healthy. You've probably seen the food pyramid, a triangle-shaped diagram that shows how much of each food group you should eat every day. And you've probably heard people talking about organic foods. There are a lot of food buzzwords, and it can be difficult to know exactly what everything means.

Instead of trying to memorize everything or getting obsessive over what you're eating, try to eat fruits and vegetables daily, on top of the other healthy foods you love. When you eat healthy, nutritious foods, you are filling up your body like you would fill up a car with gas—giving it what it needs to go full speed ahead. Junk food and foods filled with sugar and salt slow you down in the long run, while foods with lots of nutrients give you a long-lasting boost.

Balance lots of fruits and veggies with dairy, protein (like eggs, meat, fish, beans, and lentils), and whole grains (like whole-wheat bread and oats). Fill your plate with foods that make your body feel good, give you energy, and help you feel satisfied.

Breakfast = A Better Day

You've probably heard people say that breakfast is the most important meal of the day. And it is! Without an early-morning infusion of energy, your brain can't function properly, and you won't be able to learn or focus as well. Your muscles and bones also need those vitamins and minerals, since they are growing every single minute.

Even if you have early sports practice or wake up a little late, take time to eat. It doesn't have to be a sit-down meal (although that's always a great way to start the day). If you're in a rush, grab something quick and easy, like a piece of fruit, some toast, and a glass of milk, before you run out the door. Having breakfast will give your whole day a boost.

Here are some other great breakfast options:

* Scrambled eggs or an omelet (Add in some veggies and salsa to make a Mexican omelet. I love salsa!)

* Oatmeal (Mix it up with fun toppings like fruit and nuts.)

* Yogurt with granola (You can add fresh fruit to yogurt, too!)

* A waffle with fresh fruit

* Whole-grain breakfast cereal with milk

* A fruit smoothie (For extra nutrition, throw in a handful of spinach or kale with some fruit, ice, and maybe a little yogurt.)

* Peanut butter on toast with a piece of fruit or cup of yogurt

Although he probably wasn't the first to say it, Benjamin Franklin, one of the founding fathers of America, is famous for writing, "An apple a day keeps the doctor away." It's a little more complicated than that, but fruits and vegetables are wonderful fuel for your body.

The Scoop on Sugar

Not all sugar is bad, but if you think of food as fuel, then you want to eat the things that give you the most energy possible. Sugar does the opposite. Even though you might feel a burst of energy after you first eat or drink something with lots of sugar, like a candy bar or soda, you eventually get a "sugar crash." Your body can't absorb and use processed sugar the same way it uses other more nutritious foods, and too much of it can make you sluggish, tired, and irritable.

It's a good idea to think about how much sugar is in the foods you're eating so you make the right choices to keep your body moving and grooving!

MYTH BUSTER: Diet Soda Is NOT Healthier

The companies that make soda try to advertise diet brands as being healthier by saying they have fewer calories. But really, diet soda is filled with chemicals and artificial sweeteners. Studies show that these sweeteners are even worse for your body than real sugar. So do your body a favor, and when you have an occasional soda, skip the diet versions and go for the regular ones. Better yet? Skip soda all together. It's really just not good for you.

Can You Guess How Much Sugar You Are Eating?

Do you know how much sugar is hiding in common foods? Match the foods on the left with the correct amount of sugar on the right and then check your answers below (you may use some answers more than once). You might be surprised just how much sugar is in some of these foods and drinks.

The Food

1. A can of soda
2. A small apple
3. A chocolate bar
4. A bag of fruit-flavored candy
5. A cup of orange juice
6. A piece of white bread
7. A piece of gum
8. ½ cup (45 grams) of broccoli
9. A small bag of flavored potato chips

The Average Amount of Sugar in Each

a. 2½ teaspoons
b. ½ teaspoon
c. 8 teaspoons
d. 1 teaspoon
e. 10 teaspoons
f. ¼ teaspoon
g. 6½ teaspoons

Ten sugar cubes are inside each can of soda!

Correct Answers

1. A can of soda / **e.** 10 teaspoons
2. A small apple / **a.** 2½ teaspoons
3. A chocolate bar / **g.** 6½ teaspoons
4. A bag of fruit-flavored candy / **e.** 10 teaspoons
5. A cup of orange juice / **c.** 8 teaspoons
6. A piece of white bread / **d.** 1 teaspoon
7. A piece of gum / **b.** ½ teaspoon
8. ½ cup (45 grams) of broccoli / **f.** ¼ teaspoon
9. A small bag of flavored potato chips / **b.** ½ teaspoon

Caffeine

Just like sugar, caffeine is a substance that stimulates your brain—it can make you perk up for a bit, but then makes your body crash. It's found in a lot of foods and drinks, like coffee, chocolate, most energy drinks, and some soda. But even though it's legal, caffeine is a drug. It's addictive, which is why a lot of adults have a cup of coffee every morning to "wake up." Their bodies and brains get used to having caffeine and eventually need it every day.

Most doctors say it's not healthy to have a lot of caffeine, and kids and teens should be extra careful to limit their intake. Too much caffeine can keep you from sleeping. Other common side effects are headaches and upset stomachs. Doctors also warn teens that having large amounts of caffeine can cause your heart to beat dangerously fast.

You don't want to need caffeine every day, and you definitely don't want to deal with the side effects or feel antsy and agitated, so it's a good idea to limit how much you have.

☆ GET CONFIDENT: Fun in the Kitchen ☆

You don't have to eat the same thing for breakfast, lunch, and dinner every day. Get creative and come up with your own meal and snack ideas. Mixing it up keeps your meals interesting and nutritious.

You could learn to make a smoothie for breakfast. I put spinach in mine with lots of fresh fruit like bananas and raspberries, and it tastes amazing! (You won't even taste the spinach, but it will make the smoothie a cool color!) Maybe you would like to learn how to make a yummy salad or tomato soup and grilled cheese for lunch. You can even try breakfast for dinner, with a mushroom, cheese, and tomato omelet. There are endless options!

Be Your Own Chef: Homemade Pizzas

Not only is cooking at home fun, but it's usually healthier than eating out. Almost everyone I know loves pizza, and it's easy to make one in your very own kitchen!

Start with a whole-wheat crust (you can get them at nearly any grocery store) and spread tomato sauce (or a white sauce or pesto, if you want to get really creative) over the crust with the back of a spoon. Then comes the fun part! Sprinkle a little cheese over the sauce and add your favorite toppings to make it perfect for your taste buds. Try precut veggies like mushrooms or broccoli. What about a Hawaiian, with some thinly sliced ham and pineapple? Or get traditional, with some basil and mozzarella for an authentic Italian-style Margherita pizza. I love putting sun-dried tomatoes on almost anything—they add a gourmet flavor.

Make sure to follow your house rules for using the oven. And if your parents help you, maybe you'll share a slice of your pie!

Diet Nation?

You probably know from TV and magazines that there are a lot of diets out in the world. But here's the thing about diets—most of them are completely unhealthy. Some say you should never have bread, and others say you can lose weight eating cookies (honestly!). With all this opposite information out there, how are you supposed to know what's healthy and what's not?

As a growing girl, you shouldn't diet unless a doctor or health care professional is advising you. You need to eat balanced meals in order for your body to grow. So even though it might seem like the rest of the world is doing it, don't let yourself fall into that trap. Treat your body with respect by feeding yourself the wholesome foods you need to be happy, healthy, and strong.

Talking About Eating Disorders

Instead of letting their bodies develop normally, some girls develop eating disorders like anorexia nervosa and bulimia. Being obsessed with food or your weight is never a good thing. Food isn't your friend or enemy. Food is fuel for your body. You are supposed to gain weight during puberty; it wouldn't be healthy if you developed and grew taller but didn't gain any weight. A girl with an eating disorder doesn't get enough food, so she has less energy and eventually stops being able to do the things she loves. Eating disorders are serious illnesses and dangerous business.

ANOREXIA

A person suffering from *anorexia nervosa* starves herself on purpose, because she perceives herself as fat, even though she isn't. Without professional help, she will develop major long-term medical conditions like heart problems, and without treatment, she could starve herself to death.

BULIMIA

A girl with *bulimia nervosa* eats a lot of food in a short period of time (this is called "bingeing") and uses extreme measures, like throwing up or laxatives, to "purge" the food out of her system. Without help, she can suffer long-term medical consequences and even wear away the enamel from her teeth. Untreated, bulimia can also lead to death.

YOU ARE NOT ALONE

If you are dealing with anorexia or bulimia (or both), or know someone else who is, you are not alone. You don't need to be embarrassed or try to handle this by yourself. Girls suffering from eating disorders often feel ashamed and try to hide their actions, so it's important that you understand that these are serious medical conditions. If you are sick with anorexia or bulimia, it's not your fault. There are doctors and other adults who care about you and know how to help. It's important that you talk to an adult and get professional treatment right away. With the right help, you will be able to get healthy and feel like yourself again.

If you think a friend might have an eating disorder, you should talk to her. Let her know that you're worried and that you care about her. But remember, you aren't a doctor, and eating disorders require real medical attention. You should talk to an adult you trust and explain why you're concerned. The most important thing is that your friend gets care and feels loved. You probably want to keep your friend's trust, but in a situation like this, it's even more important not to keep secrets and not to try to solve the problem yourself. You want the best thing for your friend, and when it comes to eating disorders, the best thing is professional help.

Move Your Body: Exercise Is Awesome

Good foods aren't the only things your body needs to be healthy and strong. You've got to move your body, too! Nutritionist Nora Lisman says, "When we move around, we increase the flow of blood to our organs, improve our digestion, and keep our heart healthy." Your muscles and bones need exercise to grow and become strong, too. And exercise even helps reduce stress (and cramps!).

So what can you do to add exercise into your life? It's not just about going to the gym. In fact, the most fun forms of exercise don't involve a gym at all. Nora says, "The trick to making exercise a part of your daily life is to make it fun and enjoyable. Put on some music and dance around for half an hour. Play a sport. Go on a bike ride with a friend. Take a walk in nature." Anything that gets your heart pumping or makes you work up a sweat is good for your body and counts as exercise.

⭐ GET CONFIDENT: I Like to Move It, Move It ⭐

What do *you* enjoy doing? Think of your favorite ways to move your body and then go out and do one of them. Have fun!

* rollerblade
* shoot hoops
* do somersaults in the backyard
* play street hockey
* jump rope
* play four square with friends
* walk your dog
* play tag with your neighbor
* do ballet
* practice your high dive
* throw a baseball
* hula hoop
* ride your bike

* swim
* do cartwheels
* play soccer
* go on a jog
* swing across the monkey bars
* hit some powder on your skis or snowboard
* play kickball at recess
* play touch football in gym class
* sprint down the sidewalk
* go to gymnastics practice
* make up some new dance moves

* go horseback riding
* see how long you can stand on your head
* ice skate
* speed walk home from the bus stop after school
* play volleyball (or beach volleyball!)
* go to a yoga class
* learn or practice tae kwon do
* play tennis with a friend
* throw a Frisbee or play a game of ultimate . . .

What Else Do You Like to Do?

Streeeeeeeeeeeetch

Stretching is just as important as exercise. It keeps your body flexible and your muscles loose. Tight muscles are more prone to injury. It's best to stretch your muscles when they're already warm, so do it after you finish your water polo game or ballet practice.

Here are three good stretches to try. Hold each position for about twenty seconds, and don't bounce! Just let your body sink into the pose. Stop if a stretch ever hurts or feels pinched. If you have injuries or medical problems, talk to your doctor before you do any kind of exercise or stretching.

QUAD STRETCH

Your quadriceps are the muscles on the front of your thighs and do most of the work when you're walking or running.

Grab your ankle and gently pull it to your butt, bending your knee. You might want to hold on to a table or the back of a chair for balance. Don't hold your ankle out; your knee should point directly down toward the ground.

CHEST STRETCH

Doing the butterfly for swim team? Or maybe you feel a little hunched over from sitting at your desk all day? This is a great stretch for the upper body and arms.

Grab your hands behind your back and, keeping your arms straight, lift them slightly, pushing your chest out.

FINGERS-TO-TOES STRETCH

This is one of my all-time favorite stretches—it helps relax your entire body! Sometimes I do this one before I go to sleep at night just to give all my muscles a stretch after the day.

Lie down on a yoga mat or rug. Extend your arms and point your toes, making your whole body into a long, straight line, and then stretch, pulling your hands away from your head and your toes in the opposite direction. You should be able to feel this in your stomach muscles, arms, chest, back, and legs.

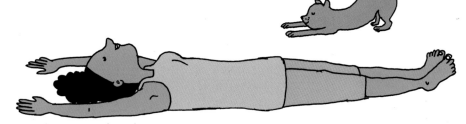

Sleeping Beauty

This very second, while you're reading this sentence, your body is growing! Your hair is getting longer, your feet are getting bigger, even your fingernails and toenails are growing. Your body is able to do all this (and much more!) without you even thinking about it. But in order to keep going, your body needs time to rest and rejuvenate.

Dr. Michele Borba is an educational psychologist and author of major books on growing up like *The Big Book of Parenting Solutions*. She says the average growing teenager needs about nine and a half hours of sleep per day, but the exact amount is different for everyone, so you need to figure out how much YOU need and stick to that. You might not be a teenager yet, but as you hit puberty, your body needs more rest, since it's doing so much growing. And your brain needs sleep, too. So if you're feeling cranky and overwhelmed, try sleeping more. She says it's also important to watch out for "sleep deprivers" like caffeine, energy drinks, cold and cough medicines, and even the computer, which can keep you up past your bedtime and prevent your body from getting real, restful sleep.

Setting up regular nighttime rituals for yourself can help you get better sleep. Try to get to bed at a normal time, and don't leave the phone or computer on in your bedroom. The bright electronic light can keep your brain partially awake, and it's hard to fall or stay asleep if you're getting phone calls or text messages. So turn them off! You won't miss anything. If you get a good night's rest, you'll be ready to talk to your friends, do your homework, and ace those new karate moves you've been practicing. You'll get the most out of your day and enjoy everything you're doing! Dr. Borba says, "One of the simplest ways to help you maintain balance is by getting enough ZZZzzzs."

Insomnia

I have a friend who can fall asleep in the middle of an action movie at the theater! But not everyone is like that. You may have heard someone say, "I can't sleep. I have such bad insomnia." Or maybe even call themselves "insomniacs." Insomnia is when people have trouble falling asleep or staying asleep through the night, and it's not fun. Most of the time, people get insomnia because of stress, anxiety, or uncomfortable sleep conditions, like when it's too hot or too cold.

If you're having trouble sleeping, think about what could be keeping you up. Are you having a hard time at school or maybe not getting along with a friend or sibling? Maybe you're worried about your history test or trying out for the basketball team. It's kind of a catch-22, because when you are worried, it can be hard to sleep, but you need a good night's sleep to deal with worries! Without sleep, the things you're stressed about can seem even worse than they really are. You just can't deal with stress as well when you're exhausted.

Talking it through with someone, like a parent or doctor, can help. Your doctor can suggest tips for sleeping better, like relaxation techniques or maybe a change of diet. You don't have to go through another sleepless night!

Having a nighttime routine signals to your brain and body that it's time to call it a day. Turn off all your electronic devices (like the TV, computer, or cell phone) at least one hour before bed and try to go to bed around the same time every night.

Girl Talk:
How Do I Stop Wetting the Bed?

Dear Sarah,
I haven't ever told my friends, but sometimes I wet the bed at night. I'm almost a teenager, and I'm worried there is something wrong with me. Do other people ever wet the bed? What should I do?
Ava

Dear Ava,
Just because no one talks about bed-wetting, doesn't mean no one else has this problem. It's nothing to be ashamed of.

The medical name for wetting the bed is enuresis (which sounds like en-yur-ee-sis). Most of the time, girls wet the bed because they sleep really deeply and have smaller bladders (the organ in your body that holds urine, or pee) than adults. While you're in a deep sleep, your body might not wake you up in time to go to the bathroom. And if you don't wake up in time, your bladder will naturally empty out.

Bed-wetting usually goes away on its own—you just grow out of it. In the meantime, it's definitely something to talk to your mom or dad about. They can help you get clean sheets on your bed and can arrange for you to talk to a doctor if needed, just to make sure nothing else is going on with your health.

A few other tips to remember:

* Avoid drinking anything for at least an hour before bedtime.

* Go to the bathroom right before you go to bed.

* See if leaving the door to your bedroom open and a nightlight on helps you wake up when you feel the urge to go to the bathroom.

And remember, lots of girls go through this.

xxx Sarah

Dealing with Scary Dreams

Your brain processes thoughts and sends out signals, even when you are in a deep sleep. Your dreams are the most vivid during the deepest stage of sleep, which is why it's especially scary when you have a nightmare.

The worst part of nightmares is that they feel very real. When you're in the middle of one, your heart can start racing, and you might even cry out or wake yourself up with a jerk.

The images and scenes in nightmares can come from lots of different sources. Maybe you saw a scary movie or read a chilling book. Or maybe you've just been worried about something and that worry is showing up in your dreams in a scary way. Sometimes your brain just processes things in your life and jumbles them together. But remember that no matter how lifelike your nightmare seems, it isn't real.

Most nightmares go away on their own after you talk about them. So instead of keeping your bad dreams inside, tell a parent or trusted adult about them. You can also try sleeping with a night-light on for a few nights or keeping your bedroom door open. Then, if you wake up from a nightmare, you'll know right away that you're in a safe place. I also like to take some deep breaths after I have a nightmare. It helps calm me down and slow that scary, heart-pounding feeling.

If you still feel wide awake after you get in bed, do some breathing exercises—count to five while you inhale, hold the breath for five seconds, and count to five while you exhale. Do this for a few breaths to help slow down your mind and get to a calm place.

CHAPTER SIX
You Are Still You!
Dealing with the Emotional Parts of Puberty

If you've learned anything from this book so far, it's that puberty is a time of change. Major change. We've mostly talked about physical changes, but there's a lot of emotional growth that happens during puberty, too. Your personality is growing—you are becoming smarter and more aware of the world around you. And you actually start thinking differently. Growing up is also about maturing emotionally and mentally, which means you are probably thinking about things in your life more.

One minute you might feel full of life, excited and happy, like a helium balloon flying and bouncing in the wind. And then, a few minutes later, you might feel like all the air has been let out of your balloon. You might feel tired or sad—you might even feel like crying. What's going on? Sure, you've cried before, but not after you've had a perfectly good day at school or when nothing is particularly wrong. The answer is, your emotions are really close to the surface during puberty. You can thank all those hormones pumping through your body!

When I was going through puberty, there were times when I felt very emotional. Sometimes I felt like crying, even though I wasn't sad or upset, and it was confusing. I remember crying one afternoon, and my mom asked me what was wrong. I said "nothing"—I really didn't know what I was crying about. She gave me a hug and told me not to worry, it was "growing pains."

She meant that it's hard, emotional work to grow up. And sometimes, because of all this hard work (and those hormones), you just need to let it out. You're going through a lot of changes, and sometimes you'll need to take a break and remember that it's totally normal to be emotional. Even with all the ups and downs, you are still you. You're the same girl you've always been; you're just adding to that girl. That's what growing up is all about—adding to the experiences you've already had and preparing yourself for new ones.

So when you aren't sure why you are feeling so up and down, remember that it's all part of the process. Growing pains really can be a pain, but they are worth it!

Dealing with Feelings

You can't stop yourself from getting emotional during puberty. But there are some things you can do to understand and deal with your emotions, so you feel more like yourself more of the time.

1) Listen to Your Feelings

Dr. Michele Borba works with teens and preteens almost every day and says, "It's normal to feel like you're on an emotional roller coaster with ups and downs. You may suddenly find yourself with a big case of the grumps and, in the next minute, running for a tissue to help hold back your tears."

Your feelings work as internal signals that will tell you how to take care of yourself. It might take a while to figure out what your feelings are saying, but be patient with yourself and try to look for patterns. Are you sad after you've stayed up late the night before? You might be tired. Do you feel annoyed with your little sister after a long day at school? Maybe you're hungry. Sometimes feeling a certain way means we need to make a change in our lives. If a friend is making you sad, for example, maybe you need to talk with them about why. When you feel emotional, take a moment to see if your brain is trying to tell you something.

2) Talk It Out

With so much going on in your life, it's important that you have someone you can talk to. Whether it's your mom or dad or another trusted adult, you need someone with whom you can share your feelings, ask questions, and turn to when you just need a shoulder to cry on! Talking about your feelings is an important part of growing up and can even help you better understand yourself.

 If you need a boost of confidence, stand up straight. Hold your head high and pull your shoulder blades back and together. Good posture is a signal to others, and yourself, that you are ready to tackle whatever comes your way.

3) Do Things That Make You Happy

There's no better cure for a case of the puberty blues than doing something you really enjoy. Painting, ballet class, shooting hoops in the backyard, or pulling out your bead kit to make a bracelet—whatever activity you like best, go out and do it!

☆ GET CONFIDENT: Growing Up Scrapbook ☆

Sometimes it's hard to see how much you've grown up because you see yourself every day, and you don't really look that different one day to the next. But you are actually changing a lot. To see how much you've grown, work on your scrapbook or start a new collage with pictures from the past few months. Include photos from your favorite activities (like going to a school play or having a sleepover at your BFF's) and hang it up in your bedroom. To everyone else it will be a cute collection of photos, but it will remind you how much you're changing and growing up!

4) Avoid the Comparison Game

Dr. Borba and I agree that "comparison is at the root of most teen angst." When you compare yourself to someone else, whether it's your appearance, your grades, how well you play sports, or who your friends are, you are never going to be happy with the results. You're different from your sister, your best friend, and the girl who lives down the street.

Comparing yourself to others is a sure way to encourage insecurity. Everyone has her own strengths. Instead of focusing on what other people do well, focus on what YOU do well.

If you're feeling down, make a list of all the things that make you who you are. Maybe you're a great friend. Maybe you're a good soccer player. Maybe you're a natural in math class. You'll be surprised how much you have to offer!

Sarah's Tip: Practice Does NOT Make Perfect

I know a lot of girls who feel like they have to be perfect, that they have to talk and act a certain way, look a certain way, and be the best at everything they do. But that's totally, utterly impossible. You might think that someone you know has a perfect life. But, even if it seems that way, it's not true. You never know exactly what's going on in everyone else's lives, and we all have something that we are working on or dealing with.

Trying to be perfect will only make you unhappy, since it's not something that you can ever achieve. So instead, try to be the best you can be. Whether you are learning a new dance or trying to get an A in English, it's healthy to push yourself and work hard. You'll make mistakes, and you might not be good at every single thing you try, but you'll never know what you're good at or what you like to do if you don't try new things. Don't let the idea of "perfect" get in your way!

5) Breathe

When all else fails, remember to Take a Deep Breath. If you are feeling emotional, close your eyes, then inhale and exhale slowly a few times. Focus on how it feels to fill up your lungs before breathing out every last ounce of air, like a leaky tire. I like to count while I do deep breathing. This just keeps the breathing even (and sometimes the counting helps me take my mind off whatever's bothering me). Breathing will give your brain a minute to refocus and will help keep you calm. It's also a great way to take a step back when you need a moment to yourself.

 **Find Your Mantra:** Having a phrase or saying that you tell yourself when you're feeling stressed can bring things back into perspective. When I'm having a hard time, I tell myself, "You are so much stronger than you think you are." It reminds me that I can do it!

Girl Talk: How Can I Talk to My Parents About Puberty?

Dear Sarah,
There's a lot going on right now, and sometimes I feel like I can't talk to my parents. I have worries and questions, but I can't even explain everything I'm feeling. I don't even know how to talk about what I'm going through.
    Leslie

Dear Leslie,
You aren't alone. It's hard to talk about your body and things that feel really personal, even with your parents. But your parents know what it's like to grow up, and they want to support you.

One girl I talked to said her parents seemed almost as embarrassed to talk about puberty as she was. That's normal—your parents are getting used to you growing up, too! It might feel awkward at the beginning of the conversation, but as things get rolling, it will get easier.

If starting a conversation out of the blue makes you nervous, try writing your parents a note. It can be easier to write out your feelings, because you have time to think about what you want to say. You can ask questions or just let your parents know what you are going through. Then you can suggest a time to talk about things in person. Being able to prepare for the conversation might make you feel a little less awkward.

You're going to have a lot of questions, because, as you say, you have a lot going on! Don't let the embarrassment keep you from getting all the info you need and most of all, remember that your parents love you.

xxx Sarah

Depression Is More Than Just Feeling Down

It's normal to feel down sometimes. Life isn't perfect, and we all have bad days, get in bad moods, and just have moments when we don't feel like ourselves. But feeling sad or unhappy every once in a while and being depressed aren't the same things. Normally, after a day or two of being upset or just out of whack, you bounce back and feel like yourself again. With depression, feelings of sadness, anxiety, or hopelessness can last for weeks, months—or in extreme cases, years. So if you feel sad or anxious for more than a couple of weeks, you need to get some help. Depression is a serious medical condition and not something you can deal with on your own.

Depression is caused by a number of factors and isn't the same for everyone. Here are some general symptoms:

* You sleep too much—meaning more than you typically do, since it's normal to need a lot of sleep as a teenager.

* You don't sleep enough, or at all, because you're anxious or worried but can't seem to pinpoint exactly why.

* You feel like you don't have any energy or that you can't, or don't want to, do anything.

* You withdraw from the things that usually make you happy, like hanging out with friends, spending time with family, or playing the piano.

* You get bad grades or stop caring about school.

* You lose your appetite.

* You eat more than normal, even when you're not hungry, because you don't feel satisfied.

* You have moments of extreme fear or anxiety, when your heart beats faster and you feel like you can't get enough air—these are called panic attacks.

* You feel like you can't live up to everyone's expectations and that you just don't want to try anymore.

* You stop caring about the consequences of your choices and become uncharacteristically rebellious.

If you recognize any of these things in yourself or think you might be depressed, you need to talk to an adult you trust. That might be hard, especially if you feel like you don't have a lot of energy or can't explain exactly what's going on. There doesn't have to be a specific reason you feel depressed. Sometimes people think it takes a hard thing, like losing a loved one or getting bullied at school, to cause depression. But that's not always the case. Depression can sneak up on you, seemingly out of nowhere.

So even if you don't feel like you can put words to how you feel, it's important to talk to a parent or an adult and share as much as possible about what you're going through. They can help you and, in the case of serious depression, make sure you get the help you need from a medical professional.

There are a lot of treatment options for depression. Some doctors use talk therapy, others use medicine, and some use a combination, and new treatments are being developed every day. Your doctor will figure out what you need so you can feel like yourself again and get back to the things that make you happy. It might take some time, but remember that you aren't alone and you won't feel like this forever. Millions of teenagers deal with depression every year, and your family, friends, and doctor can help you get through this.

A Note from Sarah:
You Are You . . .
and You Are *Amazing*

If you only take one thing from this book, I hope it's that you are amazing. When I was going through puberty, there were times when I felt like my body was out of my control. It was stressful not knowing exactly what was coming next and how it was all going to turn out. How tall was I going to get? How big were my breasts going to grow? When was I going to get my first period? There were wonderful moments and sad moments and moments when I felt totally overwhelmed. You probably feel this way, too. It's a lot to handle. Growing up is all about change, but it doesn't change the person you are. At the end of the day, you are still you, only with new skills and experiences enhancing your personality. And eventually, you will be an amazing adult. Until then, try to take it one day at a time, and when you have those out-of-control moments like I did, just remember that you are still you. And you are amazing!

xxx *Sarah*

ACKNOWLEDGMENTS

Writing a book like *Girl to Girl* takes a village—and frankly, I've got a pretty cool village. Many, many thanks to all the incredible experts who shared their time and knowledge to make this a better book, including:

* Norah Alberto, Maidenform senior style director
* Michele Borba, EdD, author of *The Big Book of Parenting Solutions* and *Today Show* contributor
* Carmindy, professional makeup artist, TV show personality, and bestselling author
* Joseph Checchio, DDS, Genesis Dental
* Rosemarie Ingleton, MD, Ingleton Dermatology
* Nora Lisman, LMSW, HC, Nora Lisman Wellness Coaching
* Elaine Plummer, RN, BNS, Tampax and Always community manager, and part of the FemCare team of health experts, the Procter & Gamble Company
* Sara Szkola, MD

Official experts weren't the only help I got. I couldn't have written this book without all the stories, questions, and advice from girls who are going through puberty now and the many girls who have been there. They are my real-life experts. Thank you, all of you! You know who you are.

My husband, Grant, is supportive and loving, and was completely wonderful during the entire writing and publication process. What can I say? I did good. He's the best husband on the planet. I was pregnant with my incredible daughter, Leigh, while I was writing this book, and thinking about what I would want to share with her one day really inspired me. I feel so lucky that I get to watch her grow up.

I also want to thank my family. My parents, Julie and David, were patient and loving before, during, and after I went through puberty. They are truly fab parents. Having three sisters and one brother meant that my house while growing up was kind of chaotic and constantly full of life. We had a lot of fun as kids and now, as adults, I'm lucky to count them as friends as well as siblings. My two brothers-in-law feel much more like brothers than in-laws and thanks to their help, I'm an aunt to the cutest nieces and nephews you can imagine. I also married into a wonderful family, all of whom I adore.

This is my third book with Chronicle Books. Sometimes I pinch myself (not too hard) to make sure that being published by them is real and not just a happy dream. My literary agent, Stefanie von Borstel, is lovely with a capital *L* and helped make this book happen. My editor, Julie Romeis, was thoughtful and kind, and her editorial guidance was nothing short of genius. I was also incredibly lucky to work with Ariel Richardson and Ginee Seo who graciously shared their energy and experience! Managing editors Ann Spradlin and Claire Fletcher were lifesavers and the wonderfully talented designer Jen Tolo Pierce and production manager Michelle Clair, who work behind the scenes to make the book both beautiful and functional, are simply amazing. And of course, I would never forget the talented sales, marketing, and publicity teams, who work to get the book out into the world. They don't get thanked enough for the energy and creativity it takes to break through the noise out there. Special thanks to marketing manager Stephanie Wong, and publicity manager Lara Starr, who have worked so hard on *Girl to Girl*.

Can you imagine this book without the artistic genius of Alli Arnold? Neither can I! Alli's warm, inviting illustrations make the book something special.

I am also lucky to have incredible, supportive friends (all wise beyond their years, of course). As a teenager, I only had a handful of friends with whom I could really be myself (thank you, Jillian). I worried that I would never have more than one or two friends who would make me think and laugh and who would really be around when I needed them. But I realize now that my high school years were just practice years for the true friends I would find as I got older. Thank you Chrissy, Amanda, Joy, Lauren, Beth, Kelsey, Allen, Kathy, Ben, and Michael. I am a lucky girl to have you all in my life.

And finally, I want to thank you, wonderful reader, for giving me a reason to write *Girl to Girl*. So please put your name right here:

- -

I hope this book is useful, encouraging, and fun, and most importantly, that it reminds you how amazing you are, no matter what's going on in your body (or anywhere else!).

XXX Sarah

 **INDEX**

A

Acne, 6–9

Anorexia, 106, 107

Antiperspirants, 40–41

Areolae, 59

Armpits
  deodorant for, 39–41
  shaving, 42, 44, 48–49

Athlete's foot, 55

Avocado conditioning
  treatment, 31

B

Bathing, 39

Bed-wetting, 114

Blisters, 54

Body odor, 39–41

Braces, 21–23

Bras
  color of, 74
  components of, 65
  first, 61, 66–67, 74
  fitting, 67–68
  history of, 67
  hooking, 66
  number of, 74
  sizes of, 67, 68–70
  types of, 70–72, 73
  washing, 72

Breakfast, 101

Breasts. *See also* Bras
  development of, 57–61
  function of, 59
  lines on, 64
  sensitive, 63
  size of, 62–63

Breathing, 121

Bulimia, 106–7

C

Caffeine, 104

Calluses, 53–54

Cavities, 18

Comparisons, avoiding, 120

Contacts, 24–25

Cramps, 92–95

Cuticles, 50

D

Dairy products, 99

Dandruff, 33

Deodorants, 39–41

Depression, 123–24

Dieting, 106

Dreams, 115

E

Ears
  headphones for, 27–28
  pierced, 27

Eating disorders, 106–7

Emotions
  dealing with, 118–21
  depression, 123–24
  moodiness, 92, 93, 117
  PMS and, 93
  puberty and, 117–18

Estrogen, 78

Exercise, 108–9

F

Face
  makeup for, 12–14
  mask, oatmeal, 15
  sunscreen on, 10
  washing, 5–8

Flossing, 19

Foot care, 54–55

Freckles, 11

G

Glasses, 24–25

Growth spurts, 37–39

H

Hair
  brushing, 29
  chlorine and, 34
  conditioning, 31, 33
  curling, 32–33
  dandruff, 33
  dry, 32
  ingrown, 49
  on legs, 42–49
  oily, 32, 33
  pubic, 77–78
  removal creams, 47
  shaving, 42–49
  split ends, 33
  static cling, 32
  underarm, 42, 44, 48–49
  washing, 28–29
Hands, washing, 52
Hangnails, 53
Headphones, 27–28
Hormones, 3, 37, 63, 78,
  92–93, 117

I

Insomnia, 113

L

Late bloomers, 3, 61

Legs, shaving, 42–49

Lice, 35

Lip balm, 20

Lip gloss, 13

M

Makeup, 12–14

Meal planning, 104

Menstruation. *See* Period

Moles, 12

Moodiness, 92, 93, 117

Music, listening to, 27–28

N

Nails
  biting, 52–53
  cuticles, 50
  growth of, 53
  hang-, 53
  ingrown, 54
  polishing, 51
  scrubbing, 50
  trimming, 50, 54

Nightmares, 115

Nutrition, 99–101

O

Oatmeal face mask, 15

P

Pads, 85–86

Panty liners, 85

Parents, talking to, 119, 122

Perfectionism, 121

Period
  bathing and showering
    during, 97
  cycle, 82
  description of, 81–82
  feminine hygiene
    products for, 85–92
  first, 77, 81, 83–85
  flow, 82
  length of, 81
  at night, 96
  preparedness kit, 87
  as rite of passage, 77
  side effects during, 92–95
  swimming during, 96
Piercings, 27
Pimples, 6–9
Pizza, homemade, 105

PMS (premenstrual syndrome), 93

Positive attitude, importance of, 35

Posture, 119

Puberty
  age at, 3, 60–61
  body changes during, 38–39
  emotions and, 117–18
  hormones and, 3, 37, 63, 78, 92–93, 117
  length of, 3
  talking to parents about, 122

Pubic hair, 77–78

R

Retainers, 22

S

Scrapbooks, 120

Shaving, 42–49

Shoes, 54, 55

Skin care, 5–8, 15

Sleep
  amount of, 111
  bed-wetting during, 114
  heavy period during, 96
  importance of, 111
  lack of, 111, 113
  nightmares during, 115
  nighttime rituals for, 113
  position for, 63

Smiling, 35

Soda
  caffeine in, 104
  diet, 102
  sugar in, 103

Stress, 35, 108, 113, 121

Stretching, 95, 110–11

Stretch marks, 64

Sugar, 102–3

Sunscreen, 10–11

Sweating, 39, 40–41

Swimming, 34, 96

T

Tampons, 88–92

Tanning, 10–11

Teeth
  braces, 21–23
  brushing, 16–18
  flossing, 19
  whitening, 20

Touching, inappropriate, 75

Toxic Shock Syndrome (TSS), 92

V

Vagina
  discharge from, 78–79
  smell from, 78, 80
  washing, 79

W

Warts, 54

Z

Zits, 6–9